ASSASSINATION
IN OUR TIME

Sandy Lesberg

ASSASSINATION
IN OUR TIME

FIRST PUBLISHED 1976 BY
PEEBLES PRESS INTERNATIONAL
12 Thayer St., London W1M 5LD
10 Columbus Circle, New York, N.Y. 10019

Designed by Nicolai Canetti

© Peebles Press International (Europe) Ltd
ISBN 0-672-52262-4
Library of Congress Catalogue No. 76-10528

The pictures on page 196 are reprinted from THE COMPLETE BOLIVIAN DIARIES OF
CHE GUEVARA AND OTHER CAPTURED DOCUMENTS copyright by Stein and Day Inc.

Distributed by
The Bobbs-Merrill Co. Inc.
4300 West 62nd St. Indianapolis, Indiana 46268, U.S.A.
in the United States and Canada

WHS Distributors
Euston St., Freemen's Common, Leicester, LE2 7SS, England
in the U.K. Ireland, Australia, New Zealand and South Africa

Printed and bound in the U.K. by
Redwood Burn Limited, Trowbridge and Esher

CONTENTS

ARCHDUKE FRANCIS FERDINAND

Born December 18, 1863 Graz, Austria
Died June 28, 1914 Sarajevo, Bosnia-Herzegovinia (Yugoslavia)

The heir-apparent to the Austro-Hungarian Empire of the Hapsburg's, Archduke Francis Ferdinand's assassination, though not the cause, was the immediate event which led Europe into World War I

Assassination conspiracy included:
Gavrilo Princip, principal assassin, 19-year-old student
Nedeljko Cabrinovic, conspirator, 18-year-old student
Trifko Grabez, conspirator, student
Danilo Ilic, conspirator, teacher
Cvetko Popovic, conspirator, 18-year-old student
Colonel Dragutin Dimitrijevic, aided conspirators, head of a Serbian secret society for the independence of Serbia, Bosnia and Crotia

The assassination of Archduke Francis Ferdinand and his wife on June 28, 1914, takes on greater importance in history as it touched off events which offered an opportunity for Germany to declare war and thus draw all of Europe into World War I. Had the assassination not occurred, it is likely that another excuse for war would have been found shortly after, but because of the sequence of events, the timely death in remote Sarajevo, now in Yugoslavia, has been credited as the match that touched off World War I.

Francis Ferdinand became heir presumptive to the Austro-Hungarian Empire in 1896, after his cousin and then his father died, leaving him next in line to his uncle Francis Joseph I of the ruling Hapsburg family. A severe lung ailment of the archduke's caused many to regard his younger brother, Otto, as a more likely successor, and it did not help either when he chose to marry a woman socially beneath him. His wife, Countess Sophie, though of an aristocratic family from Czechoslovakia, was a lady-in-waiting at the Hapsburg court when he married her. Francis Ferdinand was forced to declare his marriage morganatic, thus renouncing forever his wife's or their children's rights to the throne.

At the turn of the century, Europe was in a state of turmoil. Governments with expansionist policies were looking for ways to extend their borders and obtain new resources. At the same time, there were growing political pressures to throw off the despotic monarchies and old ruling classes.

The Austro-Hungarian Empire was not unique, having just annexed the territories of Bosnia and Herzegovina of the Serbo-Croatian peoples. These Balkan territories shared strong common bonds of origin, together with a traditional hatred for the Hapsburgs and any other foreign domination, having suffered under the Ottoman Empire for five hundred years.

Emperor Francis Joseph ruled his multinational empire as if by divine right. He evidently subscribed to the watchdog theory that to maintain and foment a state of disquiet and suspicion between the diverse annexed lands would best serve to preserve the empire as a whole. Francis Ferdinand viewed this policy as reckless. He recognized the Slavic ties that ran beneath arbitrary territorial boundaries, and he further recognized that any nationalistic policy pursued by one section would harm rather than help the stability of the Hapsburg empire. But even as heir, he could not convince the emperor of this, and it is unlikely that the temperamental and harsh-surfaced archduke could have accomplished much, given the times in which he lived, had he ever become emperor.

In 1913 he became inspector general of the armed forces, and in this capacity he accepted the suggestion to visit Bosnia and review army maneuvers. It is odd that the ruling family did not discourage such a royal visit, considering the Hapsburgs' firsthand experience with assassinations and the hostile nature of the territory to be visited. Francis Joseph's wife was herself assassinated in 1897 in Geneva; his brother, Maximillian, emperor of Mexico, died at an assassin's hands in 1867; the Serbian's own king, Alexander, and his wife, Draga, had been assassinated in 1903 by a nationalist group headed by "Colonel Apis" who was still prominent in official circles.

However, the archduke determined to go, and his wife insisted upon accompanying him on a trip that called for maximum public exposure in the Bosnian capital of Sarajevo.

Gavrilo Princip was just 19 years old in 1914—a bright student especially well versed in the Serbo-

Croatian nationalistic movement of his day together with a strong knowledge of anarchistic and revolutionary doctrines. Like most Serbian nationalists from Bosnia, he rankled under the Hapsburg domination of his country and subscribed to the idea of unification of Bosnia, Herzegovina and Serbia and the independence of the Serbo-Croatian people. Determining to assassinate Archduke Francis Ferdinand and strike a blow against the empire, he formed a *troika*, or revolutionary cell of three, with two other student friends, Nedeljko Cabrinovic and Trifko Grabez. Seeking other conspirators, they joined a secret society, *Smrt ili Zivot* (Death or Life), whose members were pledged to Serbian nationalism and whose rallying point was the Serb defeat at Kosovo five hundred years before by the Turks under whose domination the Serbo-Croatian peoples had suffered. The conspirators obtained arms from Dragutin Dimitrijevic, the same "Colonel Apis" who was personally responsible for the deaths of King Alexander and Queen Draga eleven years earlier, and who headed a powerful revolutionary secret society in Belgrade. Another *troika*, including Danilo Ilic, a student teacher, and Cvetko Popovic, an 18-year-old student, joined the conspirators.

Armed with their weapons—revolvers, hand grenades and cyanide tablets in the event of capture —the conspirators then stealthily made their way across the border to Bosnia and Sarajevo and set up hastily-made plans for the archduke's visit.

On the morning of June 28, 1914, Francis Ferdinand and Sophie had an extensive itinerary of visits and meetings throughout Sarajevo, including a sightseeing tour in an open-air car. After receiving mass at their hotel, they drove down the Appel Quai overlooking the River Miljacka en route to an official reception at the town hall. The conspirators were variously spaced along the parade route, which was decked out for the occasion with flags and medallions of the archduke. At 10:10 A.M., after casually asking a policeman which was the royal couple's car, Cabrinovic unpinned a grenade and hurled it at the archduke's car. It was deflected and exploded under the car following. The uninjured archduke headed on to the town hall where he learned of the injuries suffered in his entourage. Cabrinovic, after aiming the grenade unsuccessfully, jumped into the river but was soon captured.

Unnerving as this attempt was, Francis Ferdinand continued on his procession from the town hall, but a wrong turn by the driver fatefully brought the car to a stop right in front of where Princip happened to be standing. The first attempt had failed, but now Princip fired his Browning revolver twice at the archduke. The first shot went through the car door and through the Duchess' corset, mortally wounding her, and the second entered through the archduke's neck and lodged in his spine. On seeing her husband hit, the Duchess cried out, "For God's sake, what has happened to you?" while the archduke cried, "Soferl, don't die. Live for my children."

Rushed to the governor's residence, they were both pronounced dead—each still wearing amulet charms to guard off evil. In an hour and a half, both a foiled attempt and an assassination had occurred.

Princip and Cabrinovic (whose cyanide had only succeeded in burning the inside of his mouth) were questioned along with a mass of bystanders who were randomly hauled in by the police. Each conspirator, pledged to secrecy, maintained that he had acted alone, but when the stories did not tally and Princip feared innocent people would suffer, he divulged all and called upon the other conspirators to do likewise. The police netted twenty-five conspirators. Because of the youthful age of most of them, they received heavy prison terms instead of the gallows. Ilic who was older was hanged. Princip, Cabrinovic and Grabez each received twenty years at hard labor and were to fast on the 28th day of every month of their prison term. Cubrilovic, a friend of Princip's, received sixteen years; Popovic, thirteen years. Only Cubrilovic and Popovic survived their prison terms. Cabrinovic and Grabez died of tuberculosis in two years and Princip died of the same in 1918.

Immediately after the assassination, the Austrian government, in an ultimatum to Serbia, accused Serbian government officials of being involved in the plot. To the Austrians' surprise the Serbians accepted almost all of the harsh terms of the ultimatum, but Austria chose to consider the Serbian response unacceptable. Germany backed the Austrian demands while Russia supported Serbia. Once the various countries began to mobilize their armies, military timetables had to be met and an irreversible course was set. The assassination thus triggered a series of events that led to the outbreak of World War I.

Some of the conspirators lived to see the beginning of an inevitable chain of events that altered drastically the map of Europe and eventually led to their goal of Serbian nationalism and the formation of Yugoslavia □

Above: The archduke and his wife, Sophie, as they left the town hall in Sarajevo on the morning of June 28, 1914

Below: The archduke and duchess leaving in an open car for a parade through Sarajevo just minutes before they were assassinated

Gavrillo Princip, the assassin, as he was captured immediately after shooting the archduke and duchess

Police and soldiers surrounding the assassin as he was led away to prison

The bodies of Archduke Francis Ferdinand and Duchess Sophie lying in state in the governor's residence

GRIGORI EFIMOVICH RASPUTIN

Born 1871 ? Tobolsk, Siberia
Died December 29, 1916 St. Petersburg, Russia

A Russian peasant who practiced faith healing and became the most powerful force behind the Russian imperial family in the early 1900s until his assassination just prior to the Russian Revolution

Assassins:
Prince Felix Yusupov, principal assassin, a monarchist who feared the possibility of Rasputin's influence over his young wife
Deputy V. M. Purichkevich, chief organizer of the conspiracy, member of the Duma
Grand Duke Dmitri Pavlovich, conspirator, one of Czar's favorite cousins
Dr. Lazovert, military doctor who supplied cyanide in attempt to poison Rasputin
Lieutenant Shoukotine, conspirator

A Russian peasant from western Siberia, Grigori Efimovich Rasputin eventually held such enormous influence within the czar's family that he became the most powerful political force behind the Russian imperial throne until his assassination in 1916, shortly before the Russian Revolution which toppled the Romanov monarchy. The Mad Monk, as he was known to those who hated and feared him, reputedly possessed mystical powers and had an almost hypnotic control over many of those who came in contact with him.

Born around 1871, the exact date is not known, in the Tobolsk province of Siberia, Rasputin had no formal education but took up the life of the *staretz*, or wandering lay monks, who practiced faith healing. Spiritualism and superstition were as much a part of life at this time in Russia as the orthodox religion and had become almost fashionable in court society when Rasputin first arrived in St. Petersburg.

One story has it that Grand Duchess Anastasia made a pilgrimage to a monastery in Kiev where Rasputin coincidentally happened to be staying, and the czar's youngest daughter was so impressed by the *staretz's* self-ascribed healing powers that she asked him to come to St. Petersburg to help her brother, Czarevitch Alexis, who suffered from hemophilia. Whether or not this was how Rasputin gained entrance to the Romanov court, he did come to St. Petersburg in 1905 and gained a large following among the highborn as well as the poor and eventually was brought to the czarevitch's bedside. Alexis seemed to improve greatly under his care, thus earning for Rasputin the gratitude, then the confidence, of Czarina Alexandra, who had almost withdrawn from court life over anxiety for her youngest child and only son. Having ingratiated himself with the czar's wife, Rasputin began his ascent to power.

Rasputin seemed to be a contradiction of good and evil. He claimed to be divinely inspired and able to perform miracles, yet teaching that this healing came from physical contact with his own person was a convenient means of seducing his female followers in the name of redemption and absolution from sin. He would lure new converts, one at a time, to his private rooms where their initiation would begin. The ritual included the women undressing Rasputin and bathing him in a tub. After seducing them, Rasputin encouraged them to get drunk and behave with total abandon and depravity. Finally, after sobering up, they were to confess their sins to the monk and receive his forgiveness and blessings. Women from the most aristocratic families waited side by side with diseased peasants to see Rasputin and receive his cure. The same man who healed the czarevitch and was the czarina's favorite, all in the name of having a direct tie with God, at the same time conducted imaginative and continual sexual orgies. He was even known to keep as many as eleven women at one time, making his home seem more like a brothel than a shrine.

The czar was not a particularly strong leader and the czarina, armed with new self-confidence and encouraged by her ever present 'adviser', began issuing many royal orders. Rasputin claimed to be the voice of the *muzhik*—simple peasantry who through their purity and closeness to the earth, it was popularly believed, spoke with a collective wisdom. At Rasputin's behest, many close advisers of the czar were removed and replaced with generally incompetent favorites of the Mad Monk.

Rasputin was free to do as he pleased without fear of reprisal since he had blanket protection from the royal family. His critics were often sent to Siberia; newspapers which printed anything defamatory about Rasputin were censored. Even orders from the czar himself were countermanded if Rasputin advised the czarina to take an opposing view.

There was growing concern and dissatisfaction within upper echelons of the military and in the Duma (the Russian national assembly elected indirectly by the people) regarding the unchallenged power Rasputin was wielding. Because of this wanton exercise in control of government, Rasputin gained as many powerful enemies as he did followers. The czarina seemed blind to this dangerous course as well as to Rasputin's reputed orgiastic lifestyle; the weak czar, whose attention was more and more drawn to military matters as World War I engulfed Europe, is said to have commented that it was far better to have five Rasputins than one hysterical woman.

There were numerous possible motives for Rasputin's assassins to want him dead, and it is likely that the conspirators as a group were moved by a combination of such reasons. It is generally assumed that Rasputin was pro-German, and even before it was officially confirmed that Rasputin had attempted to negotiate a secret peace treaty with the Germans, he posed a threat to the anti-German factions. The conspirators were mostly highborn conservatives who, in light of the turmoil Rasputin was causing in government administration, wanted to save the monarchy from the hands of the Mad Monk.

The principal assassin, Prince Felix Yusupov, had reasons which were largely personal. The son of an aide-de-camp of the czar's, Yusupov was a member of one of the noblest Russian families, the Sumarakoff-Elstens, and a staunch monarchist. At the age of 27, in February 1914, he had married the czar's niece Princess Irene of Russia, and when they took up court life, Yusupov began to fear the possibility that Rasputin's mesmeric powers might lead to the seduction of his young and beautiful bride.

Yusupov determined to form a conspiracy to put a final end to Rasputin's influence, and was joined by V. M. Purichkevitch, a deputy in the Duma, who became the chief organizer of the plot. The others in the group were Grand Duke Dmitri Pavlovitch, a favorite cousin of the czar's; Dr. Lazovert, and Lieutenant Shoukotine. The plan was for Yusupov to give a party at his home on December 29, 1916, to which Rasputin was to be invited. Though Yusupov later denied using his wife as "bait", it is probable that the conspirators hoped Rasputin would come, believing that Princess Irene, whom he had never met, would be at the party. (She was, in fact, away from St. Petersburg at the time of the party.)

With his many enemies, Rasputin had been warned repeatedly to be on guard against possible attacks on his life. His own daughters, Maria and Varara, had begged him not to attend the prince's party, and it is said they even hid his boots before the party, in an effort to keep him safely at home. In spite of these efforts Rasputin came to the party at Corokhovaya Street.

The conspirators had prepared highly poisonous refreshments for the monk: the cyanide supplied by Dr. Lazovert was mixed in the cakes, used to spike the Madeira wine and even used as a rinse for the dishes on which the food was served. Yusupov watched confounded as the Mad Monk proceeded to eat up all the cakes and drink glass after glass of Madeira with seemingly not the slightest ill effect. Poison in such dosage should have been instantly fatal in almost all cases. But unknown to the conspirators, Rasputin suffered from dyspepsia, a disease where the hydrochloric acid (which must be present to activate cyanide) is not secreted by the stomach—thus the poison had no effect on Rasputin. The frantic prince then managed to distract his guest long enough to pull his service revolver and fire a bullet into Rasputin's side. To Yusupov's horror, not only did Rasputin still refuse to succumb, but the monk lunged at the prince and got a strangle hold on his throat.

Hearing the commotion, the other conspirators came rushing in to find Yusupov fleeing for his life into the courtyard with Rasputin, though weak from his wound, in determined pursuit. The grand duke shot Rasputin in the chest, and to be certain he was dead, the prince beat his body repeatedly with an iron bar. Even in death Rasputin seemed to be exerting his mesmeric powers as an unseeing eye stared back at the assassins. They wrapped the body in a fur coat and had it driven to the River Neva where it was pushed through a hole in the ice. Two policemen who were drawn by the disturbance in the courtyard were handsomely paid for their silence (1,000 rubles), but the body was recovered and much of the story pieced together.

No action, however, was taken against the conspirators.

The circumstances of Rasputin's death as well as several earlier attempts on his life (one involving a stabbing with a twenty-one inch bladed knife) have contributed to the notion that Rasputin was incapable of being killed. Whether or not his mystical powers gave him some super-human protection, it is obvious that it was no easy task for his assassins to snuff out his life.

Yusupov and his wife left Russia soon after the assassination as the threat of revolution loomed. During his long life Yusupov, among other things, practiced faith healing before he died in 1967 at the age of 81 in New York City.

In 1917 the Revolution toppled the Romanov empire, and the czar and his family, who were held in virtual captivity for the last several months of their lives, were quietly but brutally executed in Ekaterinburg. Rasputin is said to have foretold that should he die, his death would be followed shortly by that of the whole imperial family. Whether by coincidence or by divine design, events certainly proved him right□

Above: The Russian imperial family strolling on the palace grounds

Below: The czar surrounded by his family (L–R) Grand Duchesses Olga and Maria, the czarina, Grand Duchess Anastasia, Czarevitch Alexis, Grand Duchess Tatiana

Czar Nicholas II

Czarina Alexandra and the czarevitch, 18 months old

Czarevitch Alexis is pictured here in Cossack uniform. Rasputin was introduced into the royal household to help cure Alexis of hemophilia

Prince Felix Yusupov, the assassin, and his wife, Princess Irene, on board the *Berengaria* after they left Russia

(L–R) Czar Nicholas II with Alexis and Tatiana and a nephew, Nikita Alexandrovitch

Opposite: Princess Irene Yusupov

Grand Duke Dmitri Pavlovich is pictured here with his bride, Countess Colenischev-Kutuzov at the Russian Church in Paris. Pavlovitch was one of the assassination conspirators

Rasputin's daughter, Maria, in 1935

The czar and his son, Alexis, shortly before the Russian Revolution

EMILIANO ZAPATA

Born August 8, 1879? Anenecuilco, Morelos, Mexico
Died April 10, 1919 Chinameca Hacienda, Cuautla, Mexico

Mexican revolutionary general; leader in the farmers' struggle for land
and social reforms against a succession of repressive and hostile admin-
istrations; he controlled militarily much of the southern region of
Mexico, while retaining popular support, until his assassination

Assassination organizers:
Jesús Guajardo, nationalist general whose "defection" to the Zapatist
revolutionaries was part of the plot to assassinate the revolutionary
leader
Pablo González, masterminded the plot, chief general of the nationalists
under President Carranza

From the southern agrarian state of Morelos in Mexico where he grew up, Emiliano Zapata rose to become one of the great Mexican revolutionary leaders of the people in their struggle against landed aristocracy and a government unsympathetic and openly hostile to demands for agrarian reform. Zapata—as the term Zapatismo implies—became one with the cause he fought for. Loved and respected by those common people of the land—the pueblos—he became very nearly a legend in his own time and certainly after his death.

Historians dispute the date of Zapata's birth—placing it any year from 1873 to 1883—but the most authoritative agree on August 8, 1879. Considered well-off by village standards, he worked the small amount of land he had inherited, and trained and sold horses. Even though he could be something of a dandy and liked to ride around in elaborate riding dress, the villagers respected him and endearingly called him "Miliano". Zapata was a true son of his village of Anenecuilco. Elected in 1909 at an early age to the village council, the people seemed convinced that he would not abuse their trust and would always be one of them in their efforts to hold onto their land. The villagers of Anenecuilco, as pueblos all over Mexico, had been subjected over the years to encroachments on their land rights by the large and wealthy haciendas; understanding the importance of owning and working one's own land is tantamount to understanding the importance of the trust the pueblos had placed in Zapata. It is also what lay at the roots of the revolution in the fields.

In 1910, after twenty years in office and thirty years of considerable political control, President Porfirio Díaz was getting old and the question of succession became a volatile political issue. The ensuing political upheaval coincided with a growing revolt in the fields throughout Mexico, thus marking the beginning of the decade-long Mexican Revolution.

In the same year, after one of the large hacienda owners had dispossessed many of his fellow villagers of their land, Zapata took up the challenge and armed his people. In a bloodless confrontation, the land was taken back and Zapata assumed responsibility for redistributing the land among the people, settling disputes fairly and justly. The successful defiance in Anenecuilco encouraged farmers all over Morelos and Zapata's reputation grew. To the government forces, he became a dangerous symbol of insurrection.

With the outbreak of the political revolution against President Díaz, led by Francisco Madero, Zapata became the supreme chief of the revolutionary movement in the south. In 1911 Díaz was ousted and for Madero, who then became president, the revolution was over—they had defeated Díaz's dictatorial regime. But for Zapata and his revolutionary followers, the revolution could not end until the agrarian dispute had been equitably resolved. Slow to carry through on these demands, the Zapatists felt betrayed by Madero who they suspected would become another Díaz, propelled only by selfish goals rather than the people's cause.

Zapata maintained the revolution in the south against Madero, who was finally assassinated, and against his successor, Victoriano Huerta. Zapata was suspicious of alliances with the revolutionary generals in the north, two of whom were Venustiano Carranza and Francisco "Pancho" Villa. After a break in 1914 between Carranza and Villa, Zapata (Attila of the South) entered into a shaky accord with Villa (the Centaur of the North). The combined revolutionary forces succeeded in ousting Huerta in 1914 and peace followed for a time. Carranza then became president in 1915, forcing Zapata and his followers to evacuate Mexico City which they had liberated after a long, hard fight and little gain. For several years Zapata continued sporadically to fight against Carranza's government forces.

In openly challenging the government, Zapata was a constant embarrassment to President Carranza who was unable to halt the rebellion. Because of Zapata's notoriety, popularity and control of a large part of the southern states, it would be difficult to have him killed without repercussions, but in the balance, allowing Zapata to continue in blatant defiance of the government was intolerable. In early 1919, Pablo González, one of Carranza's generals, intercepted a secret note sent from Zapata to Jesús Guajardo, an officer of González's, suggesting Guajardo defect. Gonzalez saw an opportunity to maneuver Zapata into his hands using Guajardo as bait. As planned, Guajardo wrote back to Zapata agreeing to the mutiny. To test Guajardo Zapata ordered him to take the town of Jonacatepec and seize some people Zapata considered traitors. On April 8, after stalling until Gonzalez could send reinforcements, Guajardo carried out his "mutiny", taking Jonacatepec in the name of Zapata and shooting the Zapata traitors to more convincingly gain Zapata's trust.

Zapata agreed to meet Guajardo on April 10 at Guajardo's camp at the Chinameca Hacienda near Cuautla to lay further plans. Rumors were reported to Zapata of a trap and he himself had misgivings about trusting Guajardo; but after years on the run as a bandit and revolutionary, he had learned to live with and subdue these feelings.

After arriving at Chinameca Hacienda and setting up his own camp outside, Zapata was invited by Guajardo to enter the hacienda and have a taco dinner with him. Around 2:00 P.M. Zapata, followed by an escort of ten of his comrades, trooped up to the hacienda gates. Guajardo's guards were lined up at the gates presenting arms as if to do Zapata honor. Suddenly the guards opened fire and Zapata fell dead. Pitifully outnumbered, Zapata's men sustained heavy losses and the survivors, unable to retrieve their leader's body, fled south.

González did his best to squelch efforts to prolong the Zapatista movement or to deify the dead leader. He staged a public exhibition of the body to convince the pueblo followers that their leader was very much dead and had not, as many of them wanted to believe, out-smarted his enemies, escaping unharmed to the hills. Stories still persisted that Zapata had been seen riding a white horse and hiding out in the countryside. Zapata's assassination, however, did not break the spirit of the Zapatista movement or the pueblos, although tenuous peace was restored in Morelos and other areas Zapata had controlled in the south. Zapatista revolutionaries remained banded together under Gilardo Magaña, his successor, receiving aid from surrounding villages.

Agrarian demands were still leveled at and ignored by Carranza, and in 1920 when General Álvaro Obregón staged a political rebellion against Carranza, the Zapatistas under Magaña rallied and overthrew the administration. Carranza was killed trying to escape. Finally under President Obregón, Zapatistas were well represented, and agrarian equality was on the way to becoming a reality. By 1927 only four or five haciendas still functioned in Morelos; planters had lost half of their land, and the pueblos owned a great percentage of the tillable soil.

If someone of lesser stature, and at the same time further removed from the people and their land, than Zapata had been leader in his stead, his death would probably have marked the end of the pueblos cause which Zapata personified and unintentionally romanticized. Instead, the assassination of this man served as an almost magnetic rallying point to hold the Zapatista generals and followers firmly resolved in the pursuit of the revolutionary goals of agrarian equality. A man of Zapata's position could only serve to make himself a constant target for envy and annihilation by those he opposed—as a mortal he was vulnerable, but through his assassination, he and Zapatismo gained immortality and a degree of invulnerability. Zapata's death became a constant reminder to the pueblos of the need for tireless vigilance against threats to their right to work their own land□

Francisco I. Madero, Jr., president of Mexico, 1911–1913

Above: Emiliano Zapata (R seated) receiving $150,000 as compensation for evacuating his revolutionary troops out of Mexico City in July 1915

Below: Zapatista troops and their families on the march to Xochimilico after peace came temporarily in 1914

General Venustiano Carranza, president of Mexico, 1915–1920

General Alvaro Obregón, president
of Mexico, 1920–1924

Gilardo Magaña, who succeeded Zapata as head
of the Zapatista revolutionary forces, shown
in 1935 as governor of Baja California, Mexico

General Obregón as president-elect in Mexico City, 1920

PANCHO VILLA

Born 1877 Rio Grande, Durango, Mexico
Died July 20, 1923 Guadalupe, Mexico

Notorious outlaw bandit early in his career; later he became a Mexican revolutionary general

Assassins:
Jesús Salas Barrazas, principal assassin, former Mexican congressman
Eight other conspirators

"I'm not a murderer. I rid humanity of a monster," stated former Mexican Congressman Jesús Salas Barrazas, the convicted assassin of Pancho Villa. Barrazas's statement was made in 1951 almost twenty-eight years after Villa's death, but the facts surrounding Pancho Villa's life and his assassination are open to as much controversy today as they were at the time of Villa's murder in 1923. The assassin Barrazas served only six months of a twenty-year sentence—reason enough for suspicions to be aroused. And Barrazas even disputed the date of the murder which he said was committed not on July 20, 1923, as the world press reported it, but on July 11.

The assassination supposedly took place about 8:00 A.M. as Villa; his secretary, Colonel Miguel Trillo, and three bodyguards drove in the early morning sun towards Villa's ranch at Canutillo some three hours away. Another two bodyguards were positioned on the running boards of the gray Dodge as the car entered Guadalupe, a suburb of the town of Parral. The assassins were well prepared; indeed, they had been waiting for days in a small adobe building that they had planned to use as the ambush house. As the car neared the fatal site a young man stepped out and raised his hat twice and there followed the rapid fire of guns. The car bounced out of control, went up onto the sidewalk and then crashed into a tree. The conspirators came out of the building and fired repeatedly at their victims. Twelve bullets entered Pancho Villa's body, ripping his intestines out, tearing his chest open and blowing one arm almost completely off. Four bullets entered his head. Pancho Villa, hero to some, monster to others, was dead.

To this day the motives for the killing are unclear: personal jealousy, political motivation, retribution for old slights. Villa's life had been so filled with deeds of viciousness and cruelty that he had many enemies anxious to speed his eventual demise.

Pancho Villa, whose real name was Doroteo Arango, was born in 1877 or 1878 in the small village of Rio Grande, in the Mexican state of Durango. His parents were poverty-stricken and worked as peasant laborers on a huge semi-feudal estate. His father died when Villa was 12, leaving him the head of the family that included his mother, two sisters and two brothers.

At the age of 17 (or 18 or 20—the versions of the story vary) Villa shot and killed the son of the owner of the hacienda on which his family worked, when he discovered that the man had raped one of his sisters. Villa fled into the Sierra Madre taking the alias of Pancho Villa, the name of a legendary bandit chief. He joined up with a group of bandits led by Ignacio Parra, and together they held up trains and stage coaches.

Villa specialized in cattle robbing from 1897 to 1909. He expanded this activity from the Durango area into Chihuahua State. The outlaws would steal cattle and horses from one region and sell them hundreds of miles away to people who made a business of dealing in stolen cattle. As his activities increased, he became more and more knowledgeable about the terrain and more and more expert at eluding the law enforcement groups sent out to capture him.

In 1909 Villa began to assault haciendas, killing some of the defenders and robbing them of valuable possessions. His name became well known in the area and his popularity among the poor increased, especially when he distributed some of the loot among them.

In 1910 Francisco Madero headed a provisional government of Mexico from within the United States where he had sought asylum from the dictatorship of Porfirio Díaz who had been "President" of Mexico for over thirty-one years. Madero was marshalling his forces against Díaz's plan to have himself "reelected" to the presidency. Abraham González was organizing the military forces to throw off Díaz's oppression and allow free elections. Villa offered González his support for the anti-reelectionists, and González readily accepted. In this way Villa's bandit life entered into its political phase. He gained a commission in Díaz's army and rose eventually to the rank of general.

Madero's revolution was successful and the corrupt dictatorship was overthrown. He did so with the assistance of a number of leaders besides González and Villa. General Pascual Orozco, a wagon master, had organized a band of miners to join the revolt. General Emiliano Zapata, in the southern provinces, joined his own anti-Díaz revolutionaries with Madero's forces. In organizational matters Madero was greatly assisted by Venustiano Carranza. The Madero revolution was successful—Madero had won both militarily and politically when free elections were held with an overwhelming victory for him in 1911. González became governor of Chihuahua State, Carranza governor of Coahuila. Villa, at President Madero's request, moved to Chihuahua City where he was asked by the president to keep an eye on Pascual Orozco, chief of the Military Zone.

In Chihuahua City Villa set up a butcher business by renting butcher shops and selling meat, much of which was supplied from herds confiscated from Luis Terrazas, who had once owned half the state of Chihuahua with its rich cattle and mining regions. Because of Terrazas's strong links with Wall Street interests and his welcoming of American investment, the Taft Administration had not been well disposed toward the Madero revolution. By March 1912 General Orozco led a revolt against Madera, and to oppose him the president turned to General Victoriano Huerta, a former supporter of Díaz, for assistance. Huerta and Villa then joined forces against Orozco. Huerta soon arrested General Villa for insubordination and the theft of a horse. Villa was put before a six-rifle firing squad. Just as the guns were being levelled at his chest, word arrived by horsemen that the execution of Villa was to be halted; President Madero had granted a last minute reprieve. He was sent by train to Mexico City as a prisoner and locked up in the Mexico City penitentiary.

After seven months in prison Villa managed to escape and fled across the border into Texas. In the meantime revolt sprang up against Madero, and General Huerta had Madero and the vice president killed. The murders were listed as "accidental".

At that point Carranza, Zapata and Villa joined forces to defeat the usurper Huerta. In the 1913 campaign Villa was able to gain complete control of Chihuahua State, and during the next two years he was responsible for hundreds of people being shot to death. Eventually sides switched again, and Carranza outlawed Villa after Villistas had attacked Columbus, New Mexico, the first foreign invasion of the United States since 1812. In retaliation the United States launched a punitive expedition, under the command of Brigadier General John Pershing, to capture the outlawed Villa. The expedition failed and by September 1916, Villa had resumed his guerrilla warfare against Carranza and his brilliant general, Álvaro Obregón.

In the years 1917 and 1918 Villa's cruelty grew as he shot to death and burned alive a number of women who he believed were out to poison or otherwise kill him. After Carranza's assassination in 1920, Villa and what was left of his forces surrendered to the new government which then bought the Canutillo estate and gave it to him and his men. Villa purchased the best available American farm equipment and bought mules, oxen and horses for the estate. During the last three years of his life he devoted himself to his farm and business interests in the town of Parral. His enemies said he ruled the estate with terror methods to keep it under his feudal control. Others viewed him as a hero of the Mexican Revolution□

Above: The bodies of Pancho Villa and his secretary, Colonel Miguel Trillo (foreground) as they were found in their car after being ambushed in Guadalupe

Below: After the assassination, the body of Pancho Villa lies on a hospital bed

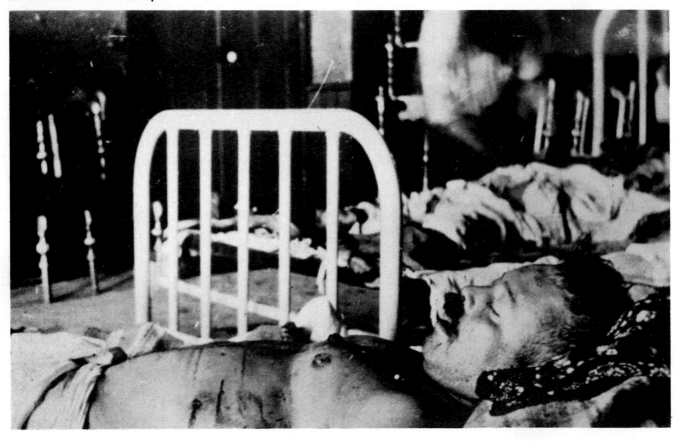

Above: Pancho Villa (3rd R) stands next to one of his gunrunners and Carl von Hoffman (3rd L), who took on-location movies of Villa for Hollywood in 1912

Below: In 1912 Pancho Villa walks away from the wall where he was about to be shot by a firing squad; literally a last minute reprieve stayed his execution

Pancho Villa, 1913

Opposite: Villa with his attorney,
Pablo Robles, at Tarreon

Below: (L–R) General Alvaro Obregőn, Villa
and U.S. Brigadier General John Pershing posed
together in 1914. Two years later Pershing
would lead an unsuccessful expedition into
Mexico to capture Villa in retaliation for
his raid on Columbus, New Mexico

Pancho Villa, 1920

Above: Villa and two of his aides at Las Delicias, 1920   **Below: Pancho Villa on the move**

AUSTRIAN CHANCELLOR ENGELBERT DOLFUSS

Born October 4, 1892 Texing, near Nank, Austria
Died July 25, 1934 Vienna, Austria

Fascist anti-Nazi dictator of Austria; Chancellor from 1933 until his assassination

Assassin:
Otto Planetta, principal assassin, member of the SS Standarte 89, the Nazi party secret strike force

On July 25, 1934, Chancellor Engelbert Dollfuss of Austria was assassinated as part of a Nazi plot to take over the Austrian Republic. The murder attempt was successful but the Nazi takeover failed; it would be four more years before the country was absorbed into the German Reich.

Dollfuss was the illegitimate son of a town laborer and a peasant's daughter; within a year of his birth his mother married a farmer and Dollfuss grew up on his stepfather's farm. From a very early age he was deeply influenced by religion and in fact at the age of 12, having envinced an interest in the priesthood, began directing his studies toward that end. When he entered the University of Vienna in 1913, he soon changed his professional goal to that of becoming a lawyer. World War I interrupted these plans and Dollfuss attempted to volunteer, but was at first rejected because of his height—four feet eleven inches. Persistence finally won him a place in officer candidate school, and he was soon sent to fight on the Italian front.

After the war he returned to the study of law and in 1922 graduated with a doctorate degree. For the next eight years he worked for the Chamber of Agriculture, meanwhile becoming active in the Christian Social party which in the 1920s and 1930s had a great deal of support from the provincial peasantry. In 1932 Dollfuss was appointed minister of agriculture, and the next year at the age of 39, he was named federal chancellor in the midst of the financial and political crises of the Depression. Dollfuss's power rested on a coalition of his Christian Social party with the small Peasant party and the *Heimwehr*, a fascist paramilitary organization which, although extremely right wing, was nevertheless opposed to the Nazis. By 1933 the Austrian Nazis had become vociferous, and Dollfuss feared a parliamentary election that might unbalance his shaky coalition. The problem of parliamentary elections was solved by getting rid of the Parliament.

The change occurred in March of 1933 when a vote of censure against the Dollfuss government came up before the Parliament. One of the Social Democrats had to leave the room for a few minutes; in the interim one of his colleagues voted in his place but marked the ballot incorrectly. When the Speaker of the House noted the irregularity in voting, an argument arose and the Speaker resigned as president of the Assembly. A second, then a third president was designated and in each case resigned. In the turmoil the last president forgot to close the session. Only a Speaker of the House could convoke a parliamentary session, and Dollfuss stepped into the situation by declaring that the Parliament had eliminated itself. Thus Dollfuss instituted his fascist dictatorship. He put into effect a 1917 law that gave him enormous powers. Public meetings and demonstrations were banned and newspapers were strictly censored.

In the field of foreign affairs Dollfuss's main problem was his neighbor to the north, Germany —Nazi Germany. To gain some sense of security for his regime, Dollfuss turned to Mussolini as a protector of Austrian territorial integrity. Domestically, Dollfuss set up a fascist one-party state somewhat resembling Italian fascism except that it had the full backing of the Catholic Church. Public support for the regime was to be expressed through an organization known as the "Fatherland Front".

On October 3, 1933, a former soldier named Rudolf Dertil made the first assassination attempt on Dollfuss, firing at and slightly wounding him. Dertil was supposedly a lunatic without clear political motivation, yet he confessed to being a member of the Nazi party.

When Dollfuss came to power there were a number of paramilitary organizations operating in the country. The *Heimwehr*, or "Home Guard", was a fascist paramilitary group led by discontented army officers whose anti-democratic policies had been represented in the Austrian Parliament by eight votes. The Social Democrats had their own paramilitary force, the *Schutzbund* or "Workers' Militia", led by former army officers of the pre-World War I monarchy. In February 1934 the Socialists led a revolt against the Dollfuss dictatorship; however, the Socialists were unsuccessful in their general strike which was the key to their revolutionary plan, and so their takeover of Vienna, where almost a third of the Austrian population resided, was thwarted. The revolt culminated in an artillery bombardment against the workers' apartment buildings and the men, women and children within them. The leaders who did not escape were court-martialed, sentenced and executed.

To prevent a right-wing attempt at seizure of power, Dollfuss integrated the *Heimwehr* into his own fascist Fatherland Front. Evermindful of the threat from Nazi Germany and from Austrian Nazis, Dollfuss, within a month of the Socialist revolt, joined with Italy and Hungary in the Rome Protocols, the economic and political proposals of which were aimed against Germany.

Hitler, who had gained power only a few weeks before Dollfuss, had as one of his primary goals the annexation of Austria into the German state. However, since Dollfuss had eliminated elections, Hitler was denied even the pretext of charade of a free election to seize control in Austria. Theo Habicht was appointed by Hitler as "Inspector General for Austria". From his headquarters in Munich he was supposed to organize sedition to overthrow the Austrian government. Beginning with violent propaganda beamed at Austrians, the Nazis directed their anti-Semetic, anti-clerical and anti-socialist messages across the border. The German Nazis smuggled arms and explosives to their Austrian counterparts. When the Austrians banned Nazi uniforms and demonstrations, Germany forbade German tourists from vacationing in Austria in an attempt to wreak havoc on the Austrian tourist trade. After grenades had been thrown at some policemen, Dollfuss decided to completely ban the Nazi organizations and proceeded to arrest Nazis—over one thousand were imprisoned but most of the leaders fled to Germany.

When the National Socialist party was banned, its members went underground and began to undermine the bureaucracy from within. Nazis were very active in the civil service and in the police force; all sorts of internal rivalries marked the Austrian Nazis, some belonged to the Austrian SA,

some to the Austrian SS, some wanted violent revolution, others a peaceful one. In addition to outright Nazis there were numerous opportunists who hoped to benefit from a Nazi takeover, although they themselves were not Nazis. Such a man was Dr. Anton Rintelen, a former governor of Styria, an ex-minister of education in Dolfuss's cabinet and in 1933 Austrian ambassador to Italy. The Nazis saw that such a man could be very useful for their purposes because he had not been openly identified with the Nazis and had held a number of important posts of responsibility in the Austrian government. The plot that the Nazis were formulating called for a government under his chancellorship to lend a degree of respectability to the first stages of the Nazi takeover.

By the spring of 1934, Austria was rocked by Nazi terrorist actions—power stations, railroads and telephone communications were being bombed with increasing intensity and regularity. Hitler met with Mussolini and presented him with a plan to have Dollfuss replaced by some "neutral person". Mussolini rejected the proposal. The outlawed Nazi party began to form a secret strike force, the SS Standarte 89, which would play the chief role in the coup. The nucleus of the strike force evolved from a group of Austrian soldiers who had formed a Nazi cell within the Austrian army. On June 24, 1934, at a meeting in Zurich, Theo Habicht and his chief of staff, Weydenhammer, met with two leading Austrian Nazis, Waechter and Glass, and made the decision to use the SS Standarte 89 in the overthrow of the government. The plot was to have three main objectives, all to be achieved simultaneously: the SS Standarte 89 was to arrest the entire Cabinet in the Chancellery; the president of Austria, Wilhelm Miklas, was to be imprisoned, and a task force was to occupy the radio station and announce that the government had resigned and that Dr. Rintelen had been appointed chancellor.

At a second session, this one on July 16 in Munich, final plans were laid down and the date set for the coup. It was decided that July 24 would be the day of the attack and that Austrian Nazis in the provinces would lead the revolt in their regions once they received the go-ahead from the captured Viennese radio station. Two factors snarled the well-laid plans of the Nazis. First of all, President Miklas left Vienna unexpectedly early that July for a vacation. This made it difficult for the plotters to arrest him along with the Cabinet. Second, the July 24 meeting of the Cabinet was postponed to the next day. Word began to filter out that a plot was underway, but for a variety of reasons Dollfuss was not informed until minutes before the attack.

The 150 members of the SS Standarte 89 gathered in a gymnasium near the Chancellery. Most of them arrived in plainclothes and quickly changed into fake uniforms that it was believed would put observers off-guard. The Nazis had obtained several trucks that would drive them into the Chancellery court yard. The Chancellery itself was guarded by officers who had only unloaded weapons; this ceremonial guard always changed at 12:50 P.M., and so it was planned to move the SS forces up to the building at that time. An ordinary policeman noticed the unusual gathering of people carrying uniforms and packages toward the gymnasium and notified the Chancellery. Dollfuss ended the conference and the various ministers left the building. Thus before the coup began, one of its key elements, the ability to arrest the whole Cabinet together, was foiled.

While most of the important government officials left the building, Dollfuss remained, and the question still exists as to why he didn't leave. It would have been possible for him to simply walk out the unguarded back entrance or even order a car to exit in the usual fashion. In any case the SS forces, commanded by Franz Holzweber, invaded the Chancellery. As the rebels rushed into the Yellow Salon, the room where Dollfuss had remained, one of them, Otto Planetta, pushed forward. As Dollfuss raised his hands to his face, Planetta fired two bullets at a distance of six inches. One bullet entered Dollfuss's throat, the other went through the spinal column and exited at the right armpit. Dollfuss fell unconscious with his legs paralyzed. At times over the next several hours he regained consciousness, but his requests for a doctor and a priest were refused.

During moments when he was conscious, Dollfuss, according to eyewitnesses, expressed the hope that there would be an immediate end to the violence. Dollfuss also expressed the wish that Minister of Justice Kurt von Schuschnigg be his successor. He also requested that Mussolini look after his wife and children who were then in Italy as guests of the Duce.

The Chancellery soon was surrounded by government storm troops, and a process of negotiation ensued between the SS forces inside and the government military forces on the outside. The conspirators' task force that was to have captured the radio station proceeded as they had planned and took control of the radio station, broadcasting the news that the government had resigned and that Rintelen was the new chancellor. Unfortunately for the Nazis, they did not know that in the next building there was another switchboard and broadcasting station, and so a call was sent out to disconnect the Nazi-controlled station from the transmitter. Soon police surrounded the building.

In the meantime Hitler had been waiting excitedly for word of the coup's success at a performance of *Das Rheingold* at the annual Wagner Festival at Bayreuth. Afterwards, with unconcealed delight at what he thought was a successful takeover, he ordered dinner as usual at a restaurant. The German propaganda machine went into high gear as it proclaimed the eventual uniting of Austria with the German Reich. But as word seeped through that the plot had failed, a new version of the news was prepared, and the radio denounced the "cruel murder" and proclaimed the whole matter a strictly Austrian affair. As for Dollfuss, he lingered on without medical attention until about 4:00 P.M. and died. His last pathetic words had been whispered to his captors. "Children, be good to one another. I always wanted to do only the best."

The conspirators surrendered and were tried and hanged. Planetta and Holzweber shouted "Heil Hitler" from the scaffold, unaware that Hitler, in a rage at their bungling of the job, had ordered that if any of the plotters managed to escape and entered German territory, they should be thrown into concentration camps. Habicht was replaced as ambassador to Austria. Rintelen was tried for high treason in 1935 and sentenced to life imprisonment; he was freed in 1938 by the general amnesty that Hitler forced on the Austrian government.

The aftermath of the assassination left Austria free for another four years; his successor, Schuschnigg, did not even have the limited popularity that Dollfuss had possessed, a popularity necessary to hold the country together. Germany learned much from the coup attempt; diplomacy replaced violence, efficiency replaced the haphazard style of 1934, propaganda reminded Austrians that they were really all Germans. When the German troops rolled smoothly into Austria in the 1938 *Anschluss*, they were welcomed by the Austrian people as liberators and brothers. Eventually Austria was to provide more than half of all Nazi war criminals in the Hitler drive for world domination, and to date, no Austrian war criminal has ever been convicted by an Austrian court□

Above: In London for the 1933 World Economic
Conference, Chancellor Dollfuss leaves in his
special airplane from Croydon Airport for Vienna

Below: Dollfuss reviewing the Austrian
Schutzcorps in Vienna's Heldenplatz,
April 1934

The chancellor addressing a crowd from the balcony of the Rathaus in Klosterneuberg

Above: Rudolf Dertil, would-be assassin of Chancellor Dollfuss in an attempt on October 3, 1933

Below: National troops advancing toward shell-marked Karl Marx apartments where workers belonging to the Social Democrats party lived

Above: Dapper in a derby and cane, Dollfuss is greeted by Hungarian Premier Gömbös (R) as political conferences between their two countries began in February 1934 in Budapest

Below: The chancellor in a lighter moment is shown here as a guest with the wives of Hungarian statesmen in Budapest

Above: Premier Mussolini (L), Dollfuss (2nd R) and Premier Gömbös (R) signing a pact between the three powers, March 28, 1934

Below: The chancellor with his wife and two children, Rudi and Eva, attending a May Day festival in Vienna

Dr. Anton Rintelen, Austrian ambassador to Italy, was to have been the Nazi's choice for chancellor of Austria after Dollfuss had been removed. Taken as a political prisoner after the assassination, Rintelen was finally freed in 1938 when the Nazi's gained control of Austria.

Opposite: Giving his famous two-fingered salute, Dollfuss reviews a parade with the youngest member of Austria's storm troops.

Otto Planetta, the assassin

Above: The Yellow Salon in the Chancellery where Dollfuss was assassinated, July 25, 1934

Below: Troops and a tank of the Heimwehr, Fascist Home Guard, surround the Chancellery immediately after the assassination. The SS Standarte 89 troops are still inside, cut off from escape

Above: The body of Chancellor Dollfuss
lying in state in the Chancellery

Below: Five of the chancellor's closest
friends, wearing uniforms of the
Heimwehr, formed the honor guard during
the funeral services

Austrians lifting two fingers in the special salute as the funeral cortege passes by

KING ALEXANDER I OF YUGOSLAVIA

**Born December 16, 1888 Cetinje, Montenegro (now Yugoslavia)
Died October 9, 1934 Marseilles, France**

King of the Serbs, Croats and Slovenes from 1921 until his assassination, Alexander changed the name of his kingdom to Yugoslavia as it is known today; a strong soldier-statesman who exercised full powers at his disposal in an effort to unite and govern the quarrelsome Slavic nations that had been merged into one after World War I

The Assassins:
Ante Pavelich, leader of the conspiracy, Croat separatist based in Italy
Vlada Chernozamsky, hired assassin, Pavelich's bodyguard of Bulgarian descent
Pospishel, conspirator, Croat exile based in Hungary
Raich, conspirator, Croat exile based in Hungary
Kral, conspirator, Croat exile based in Hungary
Maria Vudrasek, conspirator, carried weapons across borders into France
Eugene Kvaternick, conspirator, an associate of Pavelich

lexander became king of the Serbs, Croats and Slovenes in 1921 upon the death of his father, Peter I, of the Serbian royal house of Karageorgevich. Later named Yugoslavia, this kingdom was formed after World War I by uniting several heterogeneous territories: the kingdoms of Serbia and Montenegro, Croatia-Slavonia (from the old Austro-Hungarian Empire) and Bosnia and Herzegovina (formerly Austrian administered). The survival of this piecemeal kingdom was challenged both from within and outside its borders. The Serbs were a strongly nationalistic people who hoped to dominate the new country, relying on their own Serbian king. Fearing this domination, the Croats were not cooperative and pushed for a federalist coalition while more radical Croat groups held out for complete separation.

Meanwhile, Hungary and Bulgaria were not happy that parts of their countries had been annexed to form this new state, and the Albanians and Rumanians had large numbers of their own people now living within Yugoslavian borders. Italy had expected to receive more land than it did when the allies were dividing up conquered territory, and Mussolini favored any attempts which would disrupt the shaky unity of the new country, such as the Croat separatist movement.

These then were the problems which faced Alexander, and until his assassination in 1934, his attention was divided between maintaining the territorial integrity of Yugoslavia and building unity within his kingdom.

Quarreling between the Serbs and Croats did not abate, and in 1928, when several Croat leaders were assassinated while sitting in Parliament, Alexander dissolved parliamentary rule and assumed almost a dictatorial role in an effort to maintain control. A strong soldier-statesman, Alexander was militarily oriented, Serbian in outlook and concerned with centralizing his country. Rather than having a conciliatory effect on the people, Alexander's move served only to further arouse Serbian political factions and alienate the Croatian partisans.

Alexander's foreign policies involved negotiating treaties of alliance to protect Yugoslavia from the threat of her Hungarian and Italian neighbors. He formed the "Little Entente" with Czechoslovakia and Rumania to offset Hungary but had less success in gaining conciliations from or protection against Italy. After failing to get anything more than a friendship treaty with France, Alexander was attempting in 1934 to negotiate a treaty alliance with Germany as a last resort.

After the Croat representatives were assassinated in 1928, a number of Croat separatists had left Yugoslavia, seeking to fight for their cause with the aid of outside enemies of Yugoslavia. Ante Pavelich set up base in Italy, organizing a band of Croat exiles who engaged in terrorist tactics to keep the partisan tensions alive. Because most Croats back home were unwilling to commit themselves to the extremes that their separatist comrades advocated, Pavelich determined sometime in 1933 to draw dramatic attention to their cause. Thus began the plot to assassinate Alexander I. The first attempt, made in that same year, failed completely when the hired assassin evidently lost his nerve and never hurled the bomb meant for the king as he was supposed to. When it was learned that Alexander would travel to Marseilles, France, a second assassination plot was devised by Pavelich. This entailed using a professional killer, who was also Pavelich's personal bodyguard, Vlada Chernozamsky, from Bulgaria. And to ensure success, Pavelich had two other back-up plans, one in Lausanne and another in Versailles, in case Chernozamsky's attempt failed in Marseilles.

Meeting in Lausanne in late September, the group of conspirators crossed the French border as tourists en route to Paris. Along with Pavelich and Chernozamsky, the group included Pospishel, Raich and Kral, three Croat exiles from Hungary; Maria Vudrasek, who carried the ammunition needed, and Eugene Kvaternick, one of Pavelich's associates. Pospishel and Raich remained at Versaille while the others went on to Marseilles.

On the afternoon of October 9, 1934, after his official welcome to Marscilles, Alexander was driven in a parade along with Louis Barthou, the French foreign minister, and French General Alfonse Georges. Suddenly rushing out from the crowd of onlookers, Chernozamsky jumped onto the running board of the king's limousine and fired two shots at Alexander, who died within minutes. In the ensuing struggle, Barthou was shot in the arm and subsequently bled to death before proper care could be administered. General Georges sustained four shots, none of which was serious. Chernozamsky was set upon by the crowds and finally shot in the head; he died later the same day. Kral, who was supposed to have hurled several bombs into the crowd to create confusion and ease the getaway, evidently got cold feet and left before completing his mission.

Kral, Pospishel and Raich were all captured and ultimately received life imprisonment with hard labor. Pavelich and Kvaternick, who escaped back to Italy, were tried in absentia and given death sentences. As the assassination happened outside of their country, the Yugoslavians who were willing to revenge the death of their king were unable to do much other than to lodge a formal charge against Italy and Hungary before the League of Nations. But in 1934 no European power cared to alienate Mussolini; thus in the League's resolution of December 11, nothing was said of Italy's involvement in the affair, and Hungary received only a reprimand for complicity and negligence.

At first blush, because of the smooth transition of leadership and undisputed accession of Prince Paul as regent to the young King Peter, Alexander's assassination appeared to have little effect on the country domestically. In the long run, however, the policies of Prince Paul were to bring about marked differences in the administration, personnel and future of Yugoslavia. Born a Serb, Alexander was never able to overcome his more narrow Pan-Serbian outlook, while Paul ruled as a Yugoslav and therefore was more inclined to resolve the conflict between the Serbs and Croats. In August 1939, a Serb-Croat agreement was signed, acknowledging limited autonomy for the Croats in return for their acknowledgment and support of the national government. With the dismantling of Alexander's dictatorial system, Paul effectively replaced most of the military, administrative and political heads who held office or sway under Alexander's rule.

Conversely, Alexander's assassination brought about little change in Yugoslavia's foreign policies, largely because Yugoslavia was unable to do more than react to her larger surrounding environment as Europe was propelled inevitably towards war. Prince Paul was forced to rely less on alliances and more on neutrality with the rising power of Germany and Italy in his efforts to protect the territorial integrity of Yugoslavia. Fearing the outcome of military resistance towards the Axis powers, he felt compelled to sign the Tripartite Pact in March 1941 with Germany and Italy which at least temporarily staved off Axis intervention. Never fully in support of Paul, the Yugoslavian military used this move to provoke public outrage over the "surrender" of Yugoslavia to the Germans and Italians; shortly there followed a military coup which overthrew the regency and in fact the constitutional monarchy form of government in Yugoslavia□

Above: King Alexander waving from his parade automobile moments before being assassinated, October 9, 1934, in Marseilles, France

Below: Seconds after firing the fatal shots, Vlada Chernozamsky, the assassin, is seen still on the running board of the king's automobile as he is struck with a saber by Colonel Fiollet

Vlada Chernozamsky, the assassin

Ante Pavelitch, head of a Croatian terrorist organization and leader of the assassination conspiracy

Taken immediately after the
assassination, this series of
photographs show the angry mob
and a menacing fist beating the
assassin and a young man (in
white cap) who was mistakenly
thought to be an accomplice

The last few moments.
Alexander I is shown stretched
out on the cushions of the
automobile in which he and
French Foreign Minister Barthou
were riding when they were
fatally shot

The body of King Alexander just after death came

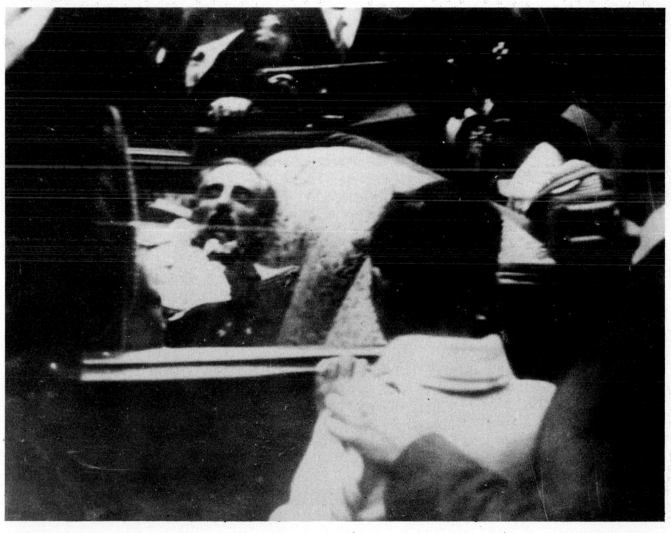

HUEY PIERCE LONG

Born August 30, 1893 near Winnfield, Louisiana
Died September 9, 1935 Baton Rouge, Louisiana

Powerful political boss of Louisiana during the Depression; governor from 1928–1930; elected U.S. senator in 1930; gained a national profile and was a presidential candidate at the time of his assassination

Alleged assassin:
Dr. Carl Austin Weiss, 29-year-old Louisiana physician

When Huey Long was governor of Louisiana, he was the closest thing to a dictator the United States had ever seen. He kept his finger closed tightly on the pulse of his Depression-wracked constituency and gave them much of what they wanted while at the same time keeping a good deal for himself. In a time when food was scarce and jobs nearly nonexistent, when Herbert Hoover was faltering as the national leader, Huey Long created jobs, built roads and buildings, fed and clothed and housed his people. That he robbed them of much of their freedom was an accepted way of life in Louisiana. He was the Kingfish, the Boss. He owned the police, the politicians, the taxes. He was, for all intents and purposes, the government of Louisiana.

Born August 30, 1893, "Kingfish", as he was popularly known, came from a humble background and grew up in an impoverished part of Louisiana, the son of a farmer. After brief legal training, he became a lawyer and soon thereafter began his career in politics. In 1928, after an earlier failed attempt, he successfully carried the rural districts to become governor. He then developed a unique concentration of political power that has been unrivaled in any state in U.S. history. In 1930 he was elected to the U.S. Senate where he mounted his Share-the-Wealth program and elevated his image nationally, much to the annoyance of Franklin Roosevelt when he became president in 1932. Under Long's control, the state government had usurped all the powers that normally resided with local authorities: tax collection, assessments, police forces, as well as most official appointments. Long himself returned from Washington to attend special sessions of the legislature which he largely orchestrated for his own purposes. It is easy to see how

some described him as a demagogue, others a social reformer.

Carl Austin Weiss was the most unlikely political assassin imaginable. He was a 29-year-old physician, a brilliant ear-nose-throat specialist who designed medical instruments in his spare time. Weiss was a good family man and had never evidenced a great degree of interest in politics, though he and his family had a strong dislike for Huey Long and his political machine. This, however, could be said of many people, both in and outside of Louisiana. Weiss married Yvonne Pavy, the daughter of Judge Benjamin Pavy, a minor political opponent of Long's. Huey Long pushed a bill to gerrymander Pavy out of his judgeship. In addition, there were rumors that Long planned to use smear tactics against Pavy and his family—implying that they were part Negro. (This allegation had been bruted about many years before and been proven to be baseless.) The possibility that Weiss heard the rumor and determined to take effective action against Long has been suggested as a motive for Weiss' actions. However, both the Pavy and Weiss families as well as many Long intimates claimed not to have heard of this rumor until after the murder.

The circumstances surrounding the assassination of Huey Long in the Louisiana House of Representatives in Baton Rouge are still in dispute, and several well-documented accounts are in direct variance. The following is the official version.

On the evening of September 8, 1935, as a special session of the legislature which Long was attending prepared to recess, Long left the chambers and walked down the corridor well ahead of his entourage. He stopped off shortly at the governor's office in the Capitol, leaving his ever-present body-guards outside. Long emerged from the office and proceeded down the pillared corridor with his guards following when Weiss, according to the inquest testimony, stepped into view and shot Long once in the abdomen with a .32-caliber automatic. Long, wounded, turned and ran down the corridor. The guards quickly set upon Weiss, disarming him and firing wildly in all directions. Weiss was dead with sixty-one bullet wounds in his body and Long died in a hospital some thirty hours later.

The only eye witnesses that testified to the killings were Long's bodyguards and close associates, and with no impartial witnesses to corroborate or contradict the testimonies, there is much room to speculate on how Huey Long actually was killed. It has been variously suggested and contended that: in the fierce firing Long may have been intentionally or unintentionally felled by one or more of his own guards; Weiss might have been disarmed by one of the guards and then his gun used to fire on Long; Weiss may or may not have intended to assassinate Long—he may have only hit him in the face and then been shot along with Long in the wild firing. (The coroner found an unexplained cut bruise on Long's mouth and Long is alledged to have said, "That's where he hit me," before he sustained the bullet shot.) It took eight days and four postponements before the bodyguards appeared at the inquest.

Whatever the real story, "Kingfish" was hated by many who considered him a real danger to the political system. He made numerous enemies who resented his success and there were many of those who would have gladly seen him dead—Long himself knew this or he wouldn't have surrounded himself with bodyguards. If not accidental, it is thus possible that someone besides the unlikely Weiss would have taken it upon himself, directly or indirectly, to commit the foul deed.

It is interesting to note that on the day of the assassination, Weiss had been perceived as acting in a calm and normal manner and had confirmed that he would carry out a scheduled surgical operation on the following day—unlikely behavior for a man planning an assassination. Weiss did keep a gun in his car and sometimes carried it on his person. Many physicians were in the habit of going armed at night, since there had been recent attacks on doctors by those seeking the narcotics and whisky carried in the doctors' medical bags. So the fact that Weiss came to the Capitol armed on the evening of September 8, 1935, cannot be used as conclusive evidence of premeditated murder.

There is much to indicate that if indeed Dr. Weiss did kill Huey Long, it was not premeditated but probably the result of his striking Long in the face and then, as the two struggled, bringing his gun into play. All his actions prior to the event point toward his positive belief that he was to live, not die. Surely had he planned to kill the closely guarded Long, he must have realized that he, too, would in all probability be killed or at least captured. Yet the day before, Weiss had bought new pieces of furniture for his home and had ordered a heating unit to be installed, telling his mother cheerfully that he was planning on staying there for at least ten more years. Whatever Weiss's motives in approaching Long, murder was probably not included.

Huey Long was the political cheap shot to whom many people responded out of desperation of the times. He made them a trade—your rights and freedom for food and jobs. I'll take care of you, he promised paternalistically, but leave the thinking to me. President Roosevelt's obviously more sound efforts to lift the country out of the Depression were in many ways embarrassed by the simple populist appeal of the Louisiana senator, and there is no way to gauge Long's personal effect on the country had he lived. But for many, he represented a clear and serious threat to the constitutional authority in the United States□

Above: The Kingfish

Below: The senator being serenaded by a "hill-billy" band

Huey Long and his wife pose in his new senate office the day he was sworn in as the junior senator from Louisiana. His first day in office, Long broke a senate tradition by smoking in chambers

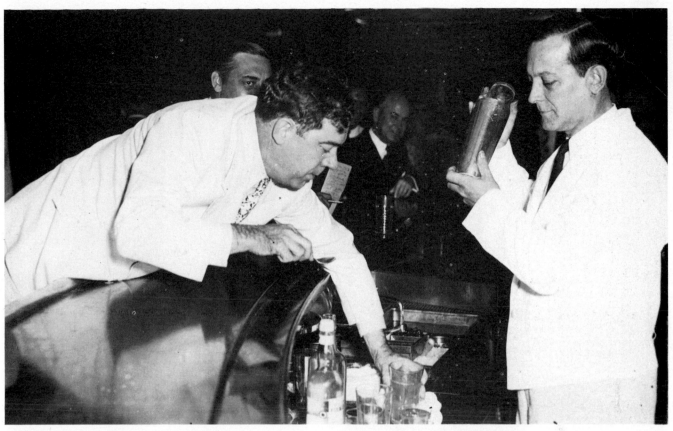

Above: An expert mixologist, Huey Long demonstrates the art of mixing "the genuine fizz"

Below: Surrounded by newsmen at a New York City hotel, August 15, 1935, after announcing his candidacy for president, Huey Long said, "Mr. Roosevelt and Mr. Hoover are bedmates of disaster"

Senator Long arriving in Washington, D.C. with his wife and daughter, Rose

Huey Long seems to take golf just as seriously as politics.

Senator Huey Long entertaining high presidential hopes at a press conference—in less than a month he would be dead

Above: Yvonne Pavy Weiss, wife of the alleged assassin and daughter of Judge Pavy

Above Left: Dr. Carl A. Weiss, the alleged assassin

Judge Benjamin Pavy, a political foe of Huey Long's

Murphy Roden, one of Long's bodyguards, at the inquest into Long's assassination, September 17, 1935. He testified that he was one of the first of the guards to seize the assassin and fire at him

Joe Messina, one of the bodyguards who testified at the inquest

Below: Mourners pass by the open casket of Huey Long in Memorial Hall of the State Capitol in Baton Rouge, Louisiana, September 12, 1935.

An aerial view of the burial service for Huey Long shows the State
Capitol which he was largely responsible for erecting and which now serves as a monument

Huey Long's widow surrounded by her children (L–R) Rose, Russell and Lamer—Russell carried on the family political tradition to become a U.S. senator from Louisiana

Mrs. Huey Long receiving a commission appointing her to fill her husband's Senate seat, from Governor James A. Noe, February 3, 1936

LEON TROTSKY (LEV DAVIDOVICH BRONSTEIN)

Born October 26, 1879 Yanovka, the Ukraine
Died August 21, 1940 Mexico City, Mexico

Russian Communist revolutionary; leading Communist theorist; creator of the Red Army; exiled from his country as Stalin gained control in the struggle for political power after Lenin's death

Assassin:
Jacques Mornard (alias Frank Jackson, Ramon Mercador, Turkov van den Dresch)

Lev Davidovich Bronstein was born in 1879 in the village of Yanovka in the Ukraine near the Black Sea. When still in his teens he had been expelled from school for becoming involved in revolutionary activities. He wrote articles, studied the works of Karl Marx and organized radical activities. As a young man he was sentenced to a four-year exile in Siberia because he had participated in a workers' revolutionary movement in Odessa. But after three years he managed to escape, leaving behind his wife and two baby girls. At the age of 25 he lived in France and Germany, returning to Russia at the time of the 1905 uprising. He became president of the Council of Workmen— only to be exiled again, this time for life, when the revolution failed. He managed to escape from Siberia after only six months, acquiring the name Trotsky from the false passport he used to get out of the country.

During this phase of his life Trotsky earned money by writing for radical publications in the countries where he lived—France, Switzerland, Austria and Germany. When World War I began Trotsky had been writing articles attacking the German socialists for their nationalistic support of Germany when he thought they should have taken an international stance. After being expelled from Germany as a "dangerous anarchist", Trotsky moved first to Zurich, then to Paris. But his radical newspaper *Our World* was suppressed and he was expelled from France. With his second wife and two children, Trotsky left Europe and sailed to the U.S. They stayed about ten weeks in New York City where Trotsky wrote editorials and articles and delivered a series of lectures.

After the czar was overthrown in early 1917 Trotsky and his family returned to Russia where he joined up with the Bolshevik wing of the socialist movement. The ruling socialist government under Kerensky favored continuing the war against Germany, but Lenin, Trotsky and the Bolsheviks demanded immediate peace. Kerensky ordered Lenin's and Trotsky's arrests, but Lenin managed to escape to Finland while Trotsky was thrown into jail only to be released two months later.

During the Communist revolution in the fall of 1917 Lenin gained supreme power and Trotsky became second in command as minister of foreign affairs. Russia thereupon ended its participation in World War I. Trotsky also became minister of war and reorganized the ill-equipped Red Army into an effective fighting force that managed in four years to defeat the various invading armies and rebel forces that fought against the Communists. Next, Trotsky turned his attention to reorganizing the railroad system, but his harsh demands turned many of the railway employees against him; Lenin relieved him of the railroad reorganization attempt in 1919. In 1923 Lenin became too ill to continue in complete control, and it looked as if there would be a struggle for supreme power between Trotsky and Stalin, who then was the general secretary of the Communist party. Trotsky's failure to return to Moscow for Lenin's funeral in 1924 was a mistake which cost him a great deal of support. Later, Trotsky was to point out that Stalin had purposely misled him as to the date of the funeral. Through intrigue and clever political tactics, Stalin then outmaneuvered Trotsky at every point so that Trotsky soon found himself divested of his powerful position in the Communist party and in the government. Lenin had foreseen the power grab that Stalin would attempt and, in his last political will and testament, had urged in vain that Stalin be removed from his post as general secretary.

By 1928 Trotsky had been exiled to Siberia. Within a year, Stalin launched a series of wholesale arrests of Trotsky's followers and banished Trotsky from the Soviet Union. From 1929 to 1933 he remained in Prinkipo in Turkey because other countries rejected his requests for admission. There he continued to write his history of the Russian Revolution which was an extended attack on Stalin.

He and his wife then spent a number of years in France and Norway, but political pressure from Stalin's dictatorship forced the Norwegian government into not renewing Trotsky's residence permit. He was invited by Diego Rivera, the world-famous mural painter, to settle in Mexico, and since Rivera was a friend of the Mexican president, Trotsky was allowed to enter the country in 1937. During the 1930s Stalin staged a series of show trials in which he rid himself of his former comrades, his past political rivals and potential future opponents. A constant stream of anti-Trotsky propaganda accused Trotsky of heading a counterrevolutionary conspiracy to overthrow the Communist government. Trotsky in turn, from a powerless position in exile, continued to denounce Stalin.

Trotsky and his followers felt the long arm of the Soviet secret police, the G.P.U., and lived under its constant threat. In 1936 professional burglars stole Trotsky's private papers that were being kept in Paris. In 1935 Trotsky's younger son, Sergey Sedov, was arrested in the Soviet Union. He was sent off to central Siberia where the G.P.U. allowed him to work for a few months as a factory engineer before executing him without a trial sometime in 1936. In July 1937 Erwin Wolf, who had been Trotsky's secretary in Norway, disappeared in Barcelona. Trotsky's elder son, Leon Sedov, died under mysterious circumstances in Paris in 1937 after being shadowed by the G.P.U. Rudolf Klement, one of Trotsky's former secretaries in Turkey and France, had been busy preparing for a congress of the Fourth International—the Trotskyite organization for world revolution. On July 13, 1938, he was kidnapped while having breakfast in his Paris apartment. His mutilated body with its arms and legs cut off was found in the Seine.

On the night of May 24, 1940, an assassination attempt was made against Trotsky at his villa on the outskirts of Mexico City. He and his wife were awakened by the sound of gunfire at close range. They hid under the bed as machine gun fire tore through the room. They heard their grandson scream from a nearby bedroom. When the five-minute attack ended the Trotskys and their grandson emerged unharmed except for a slight wound in the child's foot. Apparently the would-be assassins thought that the machine gun attack had surely finished off the family. Investigation showed that the bullets had come from different directions in a carefully coordinated plan by people who knew the exact layout of the house. Bullets had gone through the pillows where the heads of the Trotsky's would have been had they not dived to the floor. Fortunately for the Trotskys several bombs thrown into the house had not exploded. One of the guards, Robert Sheldon Harte of New York, had been kidnapped during the raid and was later found dead, his buried body covered with quicklime near an isolated house miles away. He was the eighth of Trotsky's secretaries and assistants to have died mysteriously. In Harte's case there was no doubt that he had been murdered, apparently while sleeping.

The Mexican police conducted an investigation that showed that over twenty men had taken part in the plot that was apparently directed by the Mexican Communist party. The attack was supposedly led by the artist David Alfaro Siqueiros and an unknown foreigner who spoke excellent French. Siqueiros had obtained police uniforms, the arms, and the cars necessary for tricking the guards into opening the gates, killing the Trotskys and making the getaway. There was some suspicion by the police that Harte may have been a G.P.U. member who had in turn been killed by the G.P.U. when it seemed likely that he might be caught and would talk. Trotsky himself did not believe that theory. Others have said that probably Harte had opened the gate to the French-speaking man because he must have been familiar with him, and that later Harte was killed because he would have been able to make an identification. In any event Siqueiros went into hiding and was arrested in October 1940—after Trotsky's death. He did not deny that he had been involved in the plot, but he insisted that he had given orders that no one be killed. His intention, he said, was to obtain Trotsky's documents, this despite the fact that no attackers had removed papers from the house during the raid, although they had pumped many bullets into the Trotsky's bedroom.

Within months Siqueiros was released on bail, spent several years in Chile and returned to Mexico in 1945 when it was claimed that his dossier had "mysteriously disappeared" and the statute of limitations was in effect. The French-speaking organizer of the raid was never identified.

During that same spring Jacques Mornard, Trotsky's eventual assassin, was completing the process of ingratiating himself into the Trotsky household. In June 1938 in Paris, he had met Sylvia Ageloff, the sister of one of Trotsky's secretaries. He claimed to be the wealthy son of a Belgian diplomat and pretended to be a nonpolitically minded businessman. Sylvia, a New York City social worker, became his mistress. When it was time for a vacation Sylvia went to Mexico and Mornard accompanied her, supposedly as an agent of an oil company. On May 28, 1940, he met Trotsky for the first time and did not press himself upon the household but waited to be invited. He behaved unobtrusively, brought small gifts for Mrs. Trotsky and the grandson and became familiar with the guards.

At that time there was a split among the American Trotskyites, Sylvia appearing to take the anti-Trotsky side and Mornard the pro-Trotsky side. But both were still welcomed into the Trotsky household. As the days passed Mornard became pale, his face twitched and his hands trembled. His moods alternated between grim silence and happy talkativeness. He boasted of his skill in mountain climbing and of his strength that allowed him to split an ice block with one blow of an ax. At a meal he carved a chicken with what he called "surgical skill" and also remarked that he had known Klement, one of Trotsky's murdered and hacked-up assistants. At one point he gave as his office address a location at which he could not be reached; after the assassination the street number was investigated and it turned out to be an office kept by Siqueiros. Trotsky began to express a dislike for Mornard and began to wonder aloud to his wife about the "rich boss" Mornard claimed to be working for.

On August 17 Mornard told Trotsky he had a draft of an article he would like Trotsky to go over with him. Trotsky found the meeting highly peculiar because Mornard sat on the corner of the table with his hat on and his coat clutched to his body. Afterward, Trotsky mentioned to his wife that Mornard did not seem to act like a Frenchman—despite the fact that Mornard claimed to be a Belgian brought up in France.

On August 20 at a little after 5:00 P.M. Mornard again visited Trotsky. They talked outside in the garden near Trotsky's pet rabbit hutches and then entered the house. Mrs. Trotsky offered the guest tea but he requested only a glass of water. When he was finally alone with Trotsky, he took out the pickax concealed under his coat and brought it down on Trotsky's head with all his strength. He had probably expected the victim to die without a sound, but instead Trotsky let out a piercing cry and jumped up, throwing books and other objects at his attacker. His wife returned and saw him as he leaned against the door frame, his face covered with blood. The guards jumped on Mornard who screamed that he had been made to do it, that "they" had his mother in prison. Trotsky remained conscious for periods of time over the next twenty-six hours, but finally died.

The mystery surrounding the assassin has never been cleared up. Besides the pickax, he had carried a gun and a daggar. He had written a justification of the assassination beforehand in which he expressed his disillusionment with Trotsky and that he hated Trotsky for urging him to leave Sylvia Ageloff because she was a member of a faction of the American Trotskyites who opposed Trotsky's policies. Many believe the message was contrived by the G.P.U. The assassin claimed that his name was Jacques Mornard van den Dresch; that he was born in Teheran, where his father was Belgian ambassador, and that he had been educated at a Jesuit college in Brussels and later at the Sorbonne.

An official of the Belgian Legation visited the captured Mornard in the hospital and declared that his French accent was not at all Belgian, but Swiss; that the address he gave as his own in Brussels was false; that no one connected with him, including his mother, lived at that address; that no college in Brussels bore the name of the one he said he went to, and none had a record of his attendance, and that all investigations had failed to confirm that he was the son of a Belgian diplomat.

Unfortunately his trial failed to reveal anything much about his identity. He went under various aliases such as Turkov van den Dresch and Frank Jackson. Nor was it learned what the source of his abundant money supply was. Various theories implied that he was Belgian, Russian, Yugoslavian or Spanish. Nor was it clear how he had obtained a Canadian passport under the name Frank Jackson, a member of the International Brigade who was reported missing in the Spanish American War. Some investigations into the case seem to point to his being a Spanish Communist named Ramon Mercader.

At first Sylvia Ageloff had been arrested for complicity in the death of Trotsky. She suffered a nervous breakdown and remained in a hospital for several months, but in December 1940, the Mexican court ruled that she had been arrested on insufficient evidence, so she was ordered to be freed. Mornard was sentenced in 1943 to a total of twenty years—nineteen years and six months for premeditated murder and six months for illegal bearing of weapons. The prosecution failed to connect Mornard with the Soviet G.P.U., nor was the source of his money during his imprisonment discovered. However, the generally accepted theory is that Mornard was indeed an agent of the G.P.U.; this seemed to be confirmed in 1960 since within an hour after his release from the Mexican penitentiary, he was aboard a Cuban airlines plane on his way with a Czech passport to Czechoslovakia, where he planned to take up citizenship□

Leon Trotsky, 1920

In 1923 Trotsky (L) is shown speaking before a high Soviet meeting as Stalin (R) sits listening. Political and ideological enemies, Trotsky and Stalin were rarely photographed together

Above: Trotsky, holding his son's hand, watching a parade of Soviet troops

Below: Leon Trotsky and his wife traveling by car to their home in exile in Transcaucasia

David Alfaro Siqueiros, alleged leader of the unsuccessful assassination attempt on Trotsky, May 24, 1940

Scene of the assassination attack on Leon Trotsky in his Mexico City villa, August 20, 1940

Sylvia Ageloff, a New York City social worker who became the mistress of Trotsky's assassin

Leon Trotsky, lying mortally wounded in a Mexico City hospital, August 21

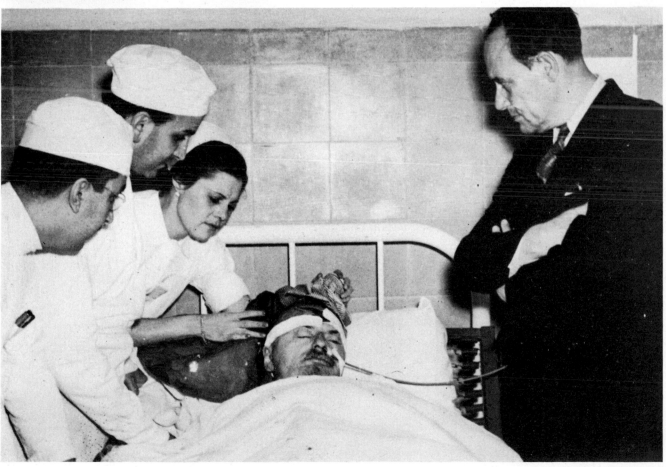

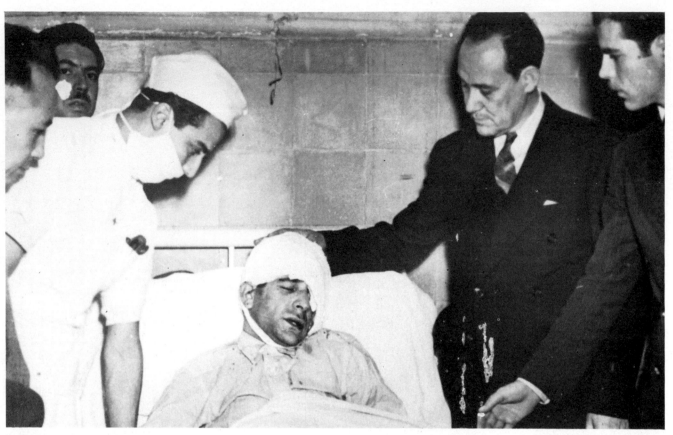

Above: The assassin, known as Jacques Mornard, recovering in the same Mexico City hospital where his victim lay dying. Mornard was beaten by Trotsky's guards before he could escape

Below: Leon Trotsky, just after death came on August 21

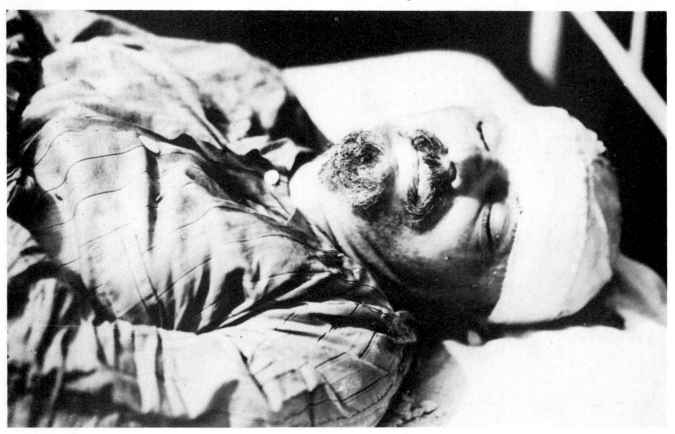

The murder weapon, a small pickax, used by Mornard to inflict the fatal head wounds on Trotsky

General Jose Manuel Nunez, Mexico City chief of police, showing the dagger Mornard had in his coat pocket at the time of the assassination

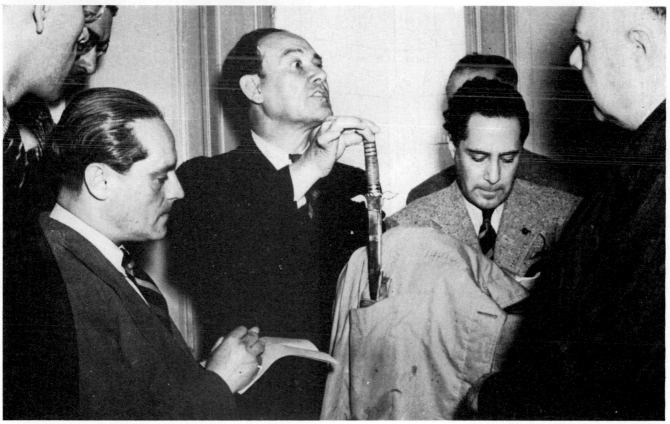

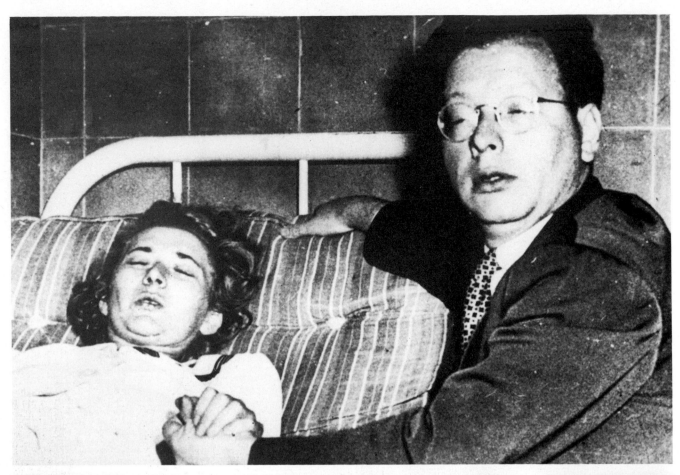

Opposite above: Sylvia Ageloff, comforted by
her brother, while being detained by police
following the assassination of Trotsky

Opposite below: The funeral procession of Leon
Trotsky, August 24, 1940, in Mexico City

In 1954, fourteen years after the assassination
of Leon Trotsky, Jacques Mornard is pictured
working at a typewriter in the radio shop of
the Federal Penitentiary in Mexico City

MAHATMA GANDHI

Born October 2, 1869 Porbandar, India
Died January 30, 1948 Birla House, New Delhi, India

Hindu nationalist leader in the struggle for independence from Britain; leading exponent of political change through nonviolence; world renowned for the moral force of his humanitarian principles

Assassins:
Nathuram Vinayak Godse, principal assassin, 37-year-old newspaper editor, member of the Mahasabha, a pro-Hindu and anti-Moslem organization
Gopal Godse, conspirator, younger brother of Nathuram
Narayan Apte, conspirator, production manager of Godse's newspaper
Mandanlal Pahwa, soldier to conspirators, sympathetic because his father and an aunt were murdered by Moslems
Vishnu Karkare, conspirator, member of the Mahasabha, restaurant owner employer of Pahwa
Shankar Kistayya, weapons carrier for conspirators
Digambar Badge, weapons supplier for conspirators, bookseller
Vinayak Savarkar, retired political opponent of Gandhi's, linked to conspiracy though not convicted

Mohandas Karamchand Gandhi was the man most responsible for achieving India's independence from Britain through nonviolent rebellion. Respected throughout the world as a great political, social and moral leader, he was above all known for his humanitarian concerns—thus to his people he was called Mahatma (Great Soul) Gandhi.

Born October 2, 1869, he began his career as a lawyer, and in his travels throughout the British empire, he experienced the demeaning second-class citizen's role of being an Indian under British rule. His creed became *Satyagraha*—active nonviolence— and his life was in every way a model of what he preached. Though he held to many early beliefs, his life was a constant evolution and refining of truths. He gave up practicing law after a time and assumed voluntary poverty. From the time he returned to India in 1915 until his death, he wore only the simple *khadi*—native handspun, woven cloth. Thus he affirmed his closeness with and support of the masses of India—even the "untouchables", those of the lowest Hindu caste on whose behalf he worked so tirelessly. The spinning wheel used in the making of the *khadi* became Gandhi's symbol for *swaraj*— home rule—as it represented India's economic independence from the empire. Gandhi was convinced that Britain's influence was causing the upheaval between Hindus, Moslems and various minorities in India, and only through withdrawal of British rule could a free India resolve these internal disharmonies.

The year 1946 finally brought the independence to which Gandhi had devoted his life. But he despaired that animosity continued to be so violently manifested between Moslems and Hindus, and that the partition of Pakistan and India in 1947 became the necessary requisite to ending Britain's presence in India. Gandhi considered this a great setback but his influence and beliefs strongly touched Moslems and Hindus alike. The enormity of the influence of this one man can be seen when frequently, in response to an impasse or communal riots, Gandhi, as a last resort, would announce a fast unto death. When this happened, both sides felt impelled to reach a settlement quickly. Yet even Gandhi, whose life manifested' such a love for mankind, had his enemies.

Holding out for Moslem and minority equality in a united country where Hindus predominated was not popular with everyone, and Nathuram Godse saw in Gandhi the demise of a Hindu state at the hands of Moslems. Godse was the editor of a Hindu nationalist newspaper and a member of the Hindu Mahasabha, an agitating organization that was violently anti-Moslem. After the 1947 partition for which he blamed Gandhi, Godse determined to eliminate Gandhi who he felt threatened the sovereignty of Hindu India. He constructed a conspiracy of seven members, several of whom like himself were members of the Mahasabha. They included: Godse's younger brother, Gopal; Narayan Apte, the production manager for Godse's newspaper; Mandanlal Pahwa who acted more as a soldier for the conspirators and whose father and aunt had been murdered by Moslems; Vishnu Karkare, a restaurant owner who employed Pahwa; Shankar Kistayya, who carried illegal weapons for the group, and Digambar Badge, a bookseller who supplied the weapons. Their preparations were slow because of difficulties in obtaining necessary weapons and devising a potentially effective plan of operation.

On January 20, 1948, their first attempt failed. At one of Gandhi's regular open-air prayer meetings, they had planned to set off an explosion, hoping to cause pandemonium and thereby giving them the chance to kill Gandhi and escape. The explosion occurred but no panic ensued, and the meeting continued as if nothing had happened. Pahwa, who had detonated the guncotton explosive, was held by a nearby woman until he was quietly arrested. It has surfaced in a 1967 inquest that Pahwa might have given police the names of all the other conspirators and that the police, with full knowledge in their grasp, did nothing to round up the group. Whatever the truth is, Godse and the remaining conspirators went free until their second and successful attempt was made ten days later.

After the conspirator's first setback, Badge and Kistayya declined a second try and Godse decided not to let his brother take part since he had a family. Apte and Karkare remained with Godse who determined to do the deed himself so that the other two could carry on the cause of Mahasabha if he were killed or arrested in the attempt.

Late in the afternoon of January 30, 1948, Mahatma Gandhi prepared to hold a prayer meeting in the garden at Birla House in Delhi (the same location where the first attempt had taken place). He walked out to the several hundred followers gathered in the garden, smiling and talking to two grandnieces who were supporting him—he was slightly weakened from a recent fast. As the crowd parted to let him pass, Godse rushed up to him, bowed quickly and fired three shots at him. Gandhi cried out "Hai Rama! Hai Rama!" (Oh God! Oh God!) Then the 78-year-old pacifist, who had devoted his entire life to non-violence, collapsed and died.

A long trial ensued during which the retired politician and political enemy of Gandhi, Vinayak Savarkar, was implicated in the conspiracy but acquitted after giving an impressive defence against any complicity in the crime.

Godse, in a ninety-two-page statement, took sole responsibility for the assassination, justifying his acts as an attempt to free Hindu India from the fanatical leadership of Gandhi and his dangerous pursuit of conciliation with the Moslem minority. Even though he maintained that he was compelled by a greater destiny to save India, Godse did not shirk ultimate responsibility for his own actions. On February 10, 1949, Godse and Apte received the death sentence; the other five were sentenced to life imprisonment. On November 15, 1949, after their appeals were denied, Godse and Apte were brought to the gallows, crying, "India united." Apte died instantly from a broken neck; Godse struggled for fifteen minutes before strangling to death.

Some might suggest that a 78-year-old man had served well his time on earth, but certainly years cannot measure the influence of Mahatma Gandhi on the turbulent world that followed his death. Strong men devoted to peaceful change are rare. Many feel kinship with the concept but are not effective as leaders. Unfortunately it would be idle to speculate on the effect of Gandhi's enormous influence on today's world; yet knowing with certitude that non-violence can achieve pragmatic results, we can with some justification keep alert to the possibility of another Gandhi coming among us. Who can deny that we need him□

Gandhi, the 78-year-old Hindu spiritual leader, in four characteristic poses

Above: Gandhi at his spinning wheel aboard the ocean liner *Rajputana* while en route to the 1931 India Round Table Conference in London

Below: Gandhi and Pandit Jawaharlal Nehru (R) participate in a *charkha* (mass spinning) demonstration held in the Bhangi Colony of New Delhi

Above: Gandhi as a young, successful lawyer

Below: A 1931 character study of Ghandi reading the morning papers

Gandhi speaking over a radio broadcasting system in a slight compromise from a life devoted to shunning devises of the modern world

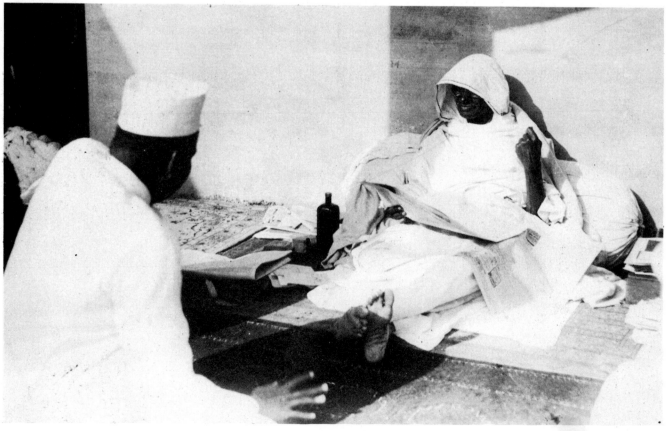

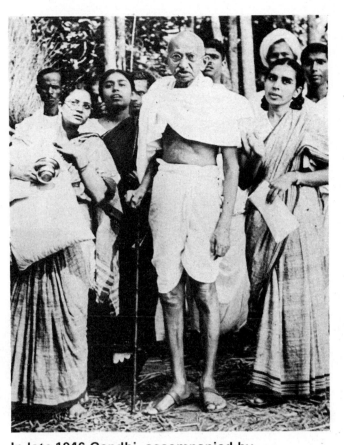

Above: Gandhi leaves London by train after failing to achieve his avowed purpose of the 1931 visit—freedom for India

Below: Maulana Azad, outgoing president of the All India Congress, speaks before handing over the reins of office to Nehru, newly elected president, at a 1946 meeting of the Congress. Gandhi is seated in the background

In late 1946 Gandhi, accompanied by Dr. Sushila Nayar (R) and Mrs. Acq Gandhi, toured Bengal Province where outbreaks of violence killed an estimated seven hundred people. The group is shown viewing the devastation

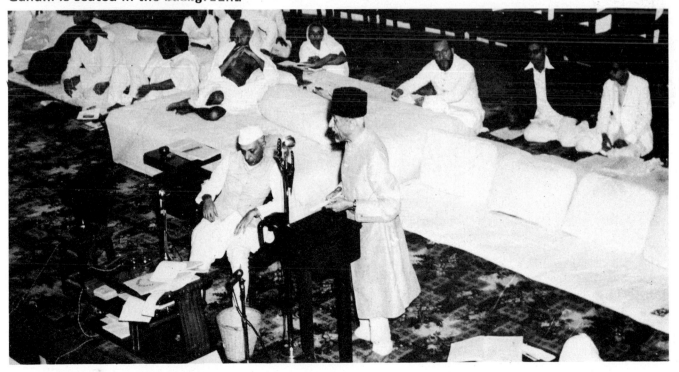

Above: Gandhi with his arms around his granddaughter, Tara, and her friend; At left is another granddaughter, Sita. Nehru is on the right

Below: Gandhi meets with Moslems during the height of the warfare between the Moslems and the Sikhs and Hindus. Gandhi marked his 78th birthday with the words: ''Today I am a lone voice in India and have lost all desire to live long.''

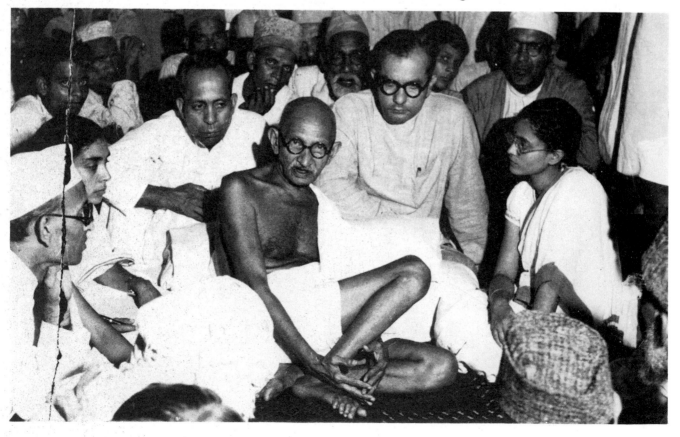

Nathuram Vinayak Godse (L), the assassin, and fellow conspirator Narayan Apte

The body of Mohandas Gandhi lies in state in Birla House in New Delhi. His granddaughters (wearing glasses) watch over him

Above: The body of Gandhi, covered with the Indian flag, in a procession leading to the funeral pyre where his body was cremated in accordance with his request

Below: High Indian officials carry the ashes of Gandhi from the train at Allahabad to the flower-decked vehicle which carried the urn to the sacred Jumna and Ganges Rivers for the final immersion ceremony over the mythical Saraswath. Nehru (center of first rank); son of Gandhi (bare-headed with shawl over right shoulder)

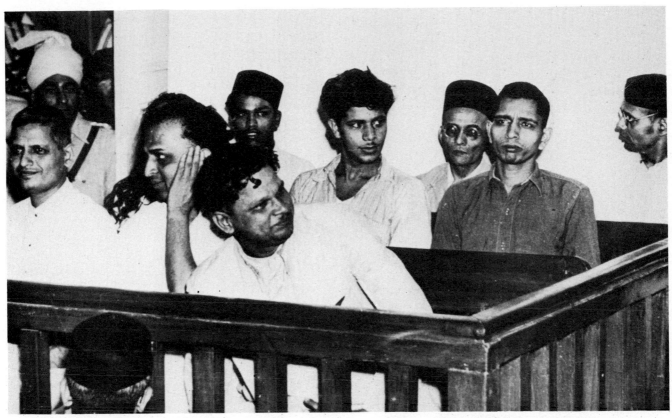

Above: On trial for the assassination of Gandhi are (L–R, front row) Nathuram Vinayak Godse; Narayan Apte; Vishnu Karkare; (second row) Digambar Badge; Mandanlal Pahwa; Gopal Godse; (back row) Shankar Kistayya; Vinayak Savarkar

Below: The architect of India's independence from Great Britain talks to his eventual successor, Nehru. Gandhi's name has become synonymous with spirituality and with nonviolent political opposition

PATRICE LUMUMBA

Born July 2, 1925 Kasai Province, Belgian Congo (now Zaïre)
Died January 17, 1961 near Elizabethville, Katanga State, Republic of the Congo

Organized his country's major political party; elected prime minister of the Congo nine days before the country gained its independence; espoused the principle of positive neutrality

Assassins:
Principal assassins never apprehended; Lumumba's political enemies are suspected for their direct responsibility

On the night of January 17, 1961, Patrice Lumumba, prime minister of the newly independent Republic of the Congo, was assassinated under circumstances that have given rise to at least eighteen different versions of the murder. Thus in death Lumumba was just as much a focus of controversy as in life when he was, at the same time, one of the most admired and most hated political leaders in Africa.

At the time of Lumumba's murder the Republic of the Congo had been in a state of chaos with military and political divisions tearing the new country apart. This state of affairs was directly attributable to the condition in which Belgium had left its former colony on June 30, 1960, when independence was declared. The Belgians had penetrated the Congo region in the last quarter of the nineteenth century, following the explorations of the American, Henry M. Stanley. During the first few decades of Belgian control, the area was in reality the personal possession of King Leopold II, under whose ownership the region was ruthlessly exploited for its wild rubber, ivory and other tropical products. In 1908 Belgium formally annexed the Congo. The Belgian policy toward the Africans has been characterized as "paternalism". The economic life of the colony was dominated by giant corporations that were carefully controlled and in some cases partially owned by the Belgian government. These huge companies were granted concessions in various parts of the vast region of the Congo, and within their designated areas they were able to operate as virtual monopolies that owned and operated plantations, mines, factories, smelters, stores, hotels, railroads, river boats, port facilities and banks. They were involved in real estate and insurance; more-over, they collected, processed and marketed the cotton, coffee, cacao and oil-palm products. All the taxes the companies paid to the Belgian government for their operations in the Congo were used by the Belgians solely for the development and government of the colony. The paternalistic system provided the Africans with elementary school education; they were protected by minimum wage laws, and although the actual cash wages were miniscule, much of their wages was in the form of free medical care, rations, clothing and housing. Neither blacks nor whites were allowed to have any voice in the government of the colony because Belgium wanted to keep complete political control in her hands—to such an extent that the mother country not only appointed the governor-general of the colony but also appointed the African tribal chiefs.

Three, sometimes competing, groups participated in the paternalistic control of the Congo and each of these interest groups had a regional sphere of influence. The administrative and transport core of the colony was located along the Congo River from the port city of Matadi to the capital city of Leopoldville. It was to this area that the Belgian government sent its directives to the governor-general. The second major interest group, the managements of the huge mining corporations, operated mainly in the southern part of the Congo in the province of Katanga, rich in copper, cobalt, zinc, tin and manganese. (The Congo had one of the only known sources of uranium during World War II.) Elizabethville, the capital of Katanga Province, was the economic core of the country. The third important interest group was the Catholic Church which dominated the enormous Congo basin, the source of wild rubber and ivory in the first decades of Belgian control. After the companies closed down in this region, the Africans in the Congo basin had their only contact with Europeans through mission stations, medical dispensaries and religious schools.

Patrice Emery Lumumba was born in 1925 and, as a member of the Batetele tribe, was brought up on the stories of Belgian atrocities: after an unsuccessful tribal revolt in 1893, the Belgians had scattered the tribe and had severed the hands of many Batetele tribesmen as punishment. Lumumba went to a secondary school which was the extent of formal education that the Belgians provided for Africans. This was because the Belgians, while encouraging Africans to become skilled laborers of all sorts, barred all but a very few from receiving a college education. Lumumba also learned from the private instruction of Protestant and Catholic missionaries. As a young man he became a militant in the Liberal Circle, a cultural society that was an off-shoot of the Liberal Party of Belgium, a party which since the nineteenth century had been opposed to the Belgian Catholics primarily on the question of schools. Lumumba worked for over ten years in the post office at Stanleyville in Orientale Province; he was eventually arrested for embezzling $2,500 and sentenced to two years in jail, but only served about one year. His supporters claimed that he had taken the money to support nationalist activities. In any case, upon his release, Lumumba got a job selling beer for one of Leopoldville's large breweries and eventually became its commercial director.

In 1956 as provincial president of the Association of Indigenous Workers of the Colony, he traveled to Belgium to study. Lumumba became known as a spellbinder who could almost hypnotize audiences listening to his speeches in favor of African nationalism and national unity. His leadership qualities led him to assume control of the National Congolese Movement (MNC) which he used as a power base to achieve national and international recognition. In 1958 he participated in the Pan-African Conference in Ghana and took up Kwame Nkrumah's idea of active neutralism, a stance that did not endear him to the Western powers. In 1959 he outlined his objectives for a national party that would stand above intertribal rivalries in the Congo. By this time the Belgians were extremely concerned about his growing popularity; the Belgian colonial police had a bulging dossier on his activities and considered him to be a dangerous individual with pro-Communist leanings. He was briefly arrested in November of 1959 but was released at the urging of the other Congolese leaders and was immediately designated as a delegate to the round-table conference in Brussels on Congolese independence.

Next he was named a member of the General Executive College which was the nucleus of the future Council of Ministers. In May of 1960 he was elected as a national deputy from the Stanleyville district to the representative body called the Chamber, and on June 23, 1960, he was selected by the Chamber to be the prime minister and minister of defense of the new Republic of the Congo.

Lumumba had gained many enemies during his rise to power. In the period before independence his main political rival was Joseph Kasavubu who wanted a Congo based on a federal system with a great deal of provincial autonomy; Lumumba, on the other hand, wanted a strong central government. Finally, Kasavubu agreed to accept the post of president of the new republic. The mining province of Bakwanga wanted politicians in Leopoldville who would favor their region and they knew that such was not the case with Lumumba. Catholics, with the support of the local bishop, accused him of Communist and pro-Soviet leanings; labor unions, upset by growing unemployment and inflation, accused the new government of corruption and demagoguery; Europeans were angered by a Lumumba speech delivered in the Chamber on independence day in the presence of the Belgian king. "Slavery was imposed on us by force," he shouted. "We have known ironies and insults! We remember the blows that [we] had to submit to morning, noon and night because we were Negroes!"

With the help of Belgian military interventions, Moise Tshombe proclaimed the independence of the mineral-rich Katanga Province in July 1960, thus presenting the Congo with a grave threat to its unity. Momentarily this action brought Kasavubu and Lumumba together in an appeal to the UN to militarily intervene in order to oust the Belgian forces in the secessionist province of Katanga. Together they also appealed to the U.S.S.R. for help and announced the break in diplomatic relations with Belgium.

In the months before and after his taking office as prime minister, many had expressed their hostility to Lumumba. One director of important colonial companies expressed the hope that Lumumba would be liquidated by a bullet through his head and volunteered to search the insane asylums in the Congo to find a madman to carry out the deed. A conservative Belgian Catholic paper denounced Lumumba's ministers as primitive savages, imbeciles and Communist creatures and published attacks expressing the hope that some of his officers might "with a single gesture . . . rid the planet of his bloody effrontery".

According to the U.S. Senate Intelligence Committee report made public in late 1975, the United States government took an equally unfavorable view of Lumumba. In fact officials of the U.S. government initiated and participated in a plot to assassinate Lumumba. According to that report, there are enough documents and testimony to reasonably infer that a plot to assassinate Lumumba was authorized, either directly or tacitly, by President Eisenhower. The planned murder was spoken of by the use of circumlocution and euphemism when speaking to the president so that the U.S. government could plausibly deny involvement if the plan were uncovered. Beginning in the second half of 1960, plans were made at the highest level to kill Lumumba. Minutes of meetings of the Special Group (an intelligence body) and the National Security Council mention plans to "dispose of" Lumumba and contain language mentioning an "extremely strong feeling about the necessity for straight forward action" and a refusal to rule out any activity that might contribute to "getting rid of" Lumumba. In the fall of 1960 two CIA officials with criminal backgrounds were asked by superiors to assassinate Lumumba, and exploratory steps were made to gain access to him. The conspiracy, authorized by Allen Dulles, Director of Central Intelligence, resulted in the sending of poisons to the Congo to be utilized by the CIA assassins, one of whom the CIA's Africa Division chief recommended as a person who "will dutifully undertake appropriate action for its execution without pangs of conscience". According to the Senate report the only reason this plan to eliminate Lumumba and have him replaced by his more pro-Western rivals was not completed was because someone else, obviously his political rivals, had already murdered Lumumba without U.S. assistance.

In July 1960 Lumumba had flown to New York to appeal to the UN for political support and assistance against the Belgian-supported Katanga government. Upon his return to the Congo Lumumba found his position very precarious. By early

September Soviet planes were to be seen in Stanleyville, the center of Lumumba's popular support, and Czech technicians were in Leopoldville; rumors spread that Lumumba was planning a coup d'état. On September 5, 1960, President Kasavubu dismissed Lumumba as prime minister, and Lumumba responded by dismissing Kasavubu. In the chaotic week that followed, Colonel Mobutu, chief staff officer of the Congolese National Army, ordered a "neutralization" of all political institutions and forbade Kasavubu, the Chamber, the Lumumba ministers and the new ministers appointed by Kasavubu from taking or initiating any activity. He vested governmental power in the Board of Commissioners which, being composed of Lumumba's enemies, promptly recognized Kasavubu's authority. Lumumba was arrested twice and escaped twice before returning to his home where he sought the protection of the UN for himself. He was kept under the guard of the UN and the Congolese National Army but managed to slip out, hidden in his brother's Chevrolet. The chase was on as he attempted to flee from Leopoldville eastward to the base of his support in Stanleyville. Traveling with him were his wife and one of his children; Maurice Mpolo, minister of youth; Joseph Okito, president of the suspended Congolese Senate, and several others. The group was captured and Lumumba, Mpolo and Okito were imprisoned at Thysville, a military encampment southwest of Leopoldville.

It was decided that the prisoners were to be transferred from Thysville. This is the point at which there is a decided divergence in the story. A decision was made to fly the prisoners to Elizabethville, capital of the secessionist province of Katanga, where Lumumba's bitterest political enemies were in control—Moise Tshombe, president of Katanga Province, and Godefroid Munongo, minister of the interior of Katanga. There is little doubt that Kasavubu had made the decision to deliver Lumumba into the hands of people who would benefit from his death. One version of the murder has it that Lumumba was beaten to death on the plane flight to Elizabethville, another has it that he was beaten to such an extent on the flight that no medical attention could have saved him. When the plane landed, Katanga military forces prevented UN forces from approaching it. The Katanga version of Lumumba's death, a version put out by Munongo in mid-February of 1961, had it that Lumumba, Mpolo and Okito escaped from the house in which they were being held, fled in a car and were killed in a remote village by hostile tribesmen. Virtually no one accepted that story and the UN instituted an investigation which came up with the following conclusions:

1. Lumumba was not killed, as the Munongo version would have it, by tribesmen on February 12, 1961.

2. Lumumba, Mpolo and Okito were killed on January 17, 1961, not far from Elizabethville and in all probability in the presence of high officials in the Katanga government, including Tshombe himself and Munongo.

3. A great deal of suspicion for the actual murder fell upon Colonel Huyghe, who was assisted by Captain Gat—both Belgian mercenaries.

4. Responsibility for the murders could also be placed directly on Kasavubu for putting the victims in a position that menaced their lives.

Eye-witness accounts exist and these vary somewhat due to a number of reasons. At first some of those involved wanted to gain the glory of having administered the final blows; afterwards they sought to deny involvement; the group that perpetrated the murders had been drinking in celebration of the capture of Lumumba and so their accounts are different; fear of reprisals certainly is always a prominent motivation for self-serving statements. Indeed, the under secretary of state for information in Katanga, according to one report, was a witness to the assassination and disappeared mysteriously in November 1961 after the UN issued its own report. It was said that he had been killed in a hunting accident.

The descriptions of the murder scene vary, but the accounts in general have the three men being killed by gunshots with Lumumba also being bayoneted. Several reports have it that Munongo administered the bayonet by slowly burying it in Lumumba's body, then the mercenaries completed the job by riddling the body with bullets or simply firing one bullet into his head as a *coup de grâce*.

The immediate reaction to Lumumba's death was one of worldwide protest against the atrocity, with mob scenes directed against the Belgian embassies throughout the world. The Soviet Union demanded Dag Hammarskjold's resignation, and Communist bloc countries accused the Western powers of complicity in the murder. The U.S.S.R., East Germany, the U.A.R. and neutralist Ghana recognized the Marxist-oriented government in Stanleyville as the Congo government. In the long run, Communist influence in the Congo was weakened. After turmoil that lasted several years the secessionist provinces rejoined the central government, and Colonel Joseph Mobuto in 1965 became the president of a strong central regime. Since then Mobuto (now called Mobuto Sese Seko) has instituted a program of Africanization and at the same time has vigorously aligned his country (now called Zaire) with the interests of the West, particularly the United States □

Patrice Lumumba (bearded, left center) being released from prison in January 1960 to enable him to participate in the Belgian-Congolese round table conference in Brussels; the meeting reached agreement on the timetable for Congolese independence which was proclaimed August 15, 1960

Joseph Kasavubu, president of the Congo

Above: The power in Katanga in 1960;
President Moise Tshombe (R) and Minister
of the Interior Godefroid Munongo

Below: Colonel Joseph Mobutu (center) emerged as
Congolese Army strongman in September 1960.
Planeloads of Russians flew out of the Congo after
Mobutu ordered the ouster of Communist diplomats

Colonel Joseph Mobutu announced that the army would take over the reins of government. Mobutu holds a picture of Soviet Premier Krushchev with lettering that says, "Hands off the Congo." Hours later Lumumba announced Mobutu's arrest

Above: Congolese soldiers fire at Baluba tribesmen as two Balubas lie dead during the September 1960 invasion by Lumumba's troops. The soldiers were sent to ''pacify'' the rebellious tribesmen. The one nearest camera was stabbed by his own spear

Below: His arms roped behind him, ousted Congo Premier Lumumba (R) had been captured by troops of Colonel Mobutu, four days after Lumumba had attempted to flee from Leopoldville to his stronghold at Stanleyville

With the knowledge of impending and inevitable death reflected in his eyes, Lumumba waits with Joseph Okito, president of the Congolese Senate, as their captors prepare to fly them to Katanga Province

According to Katanga Interior Minister Monungo, Lumumba and Okito and Mpolo escaped captivity through this hole, only to be found on February 13, 1961, killed by hostile tribesmen. A UN investigation revealed this to be an assassination cover-up story

A view of the hut and the hole through which Lumumba and his aides allegedly made their escape

Above: In Paris police rout demonstrators near the Belgian embassy, protesting the murder of Lumumba.

Below: In Bonn students wave Lumumba posters and scream, "Nazis! Murderers! Down with all Germans!" as police move against African demonstrators.

Opposite above: Patrice Lumumba, Jr. in Cairo, playing
with a toy pistol, the day before he learned of
his father's death

Opposite below: Six months after the assassination
of Lumumba, Congolese President Joseph Kasavubu (L)
and Army Chief Joseph Mobutu review troops on the
country's first Independence Day anniversary.

Pauline Lumumba, widow of the slain premier, leads
a group of mourners through the streets of Leopoldville.
Mrs. Lumumba is bare-breasted as a sign of mourning.
She sought, to no avail, to persuade the UN to have her
husband's body returned and given a Christian burial.

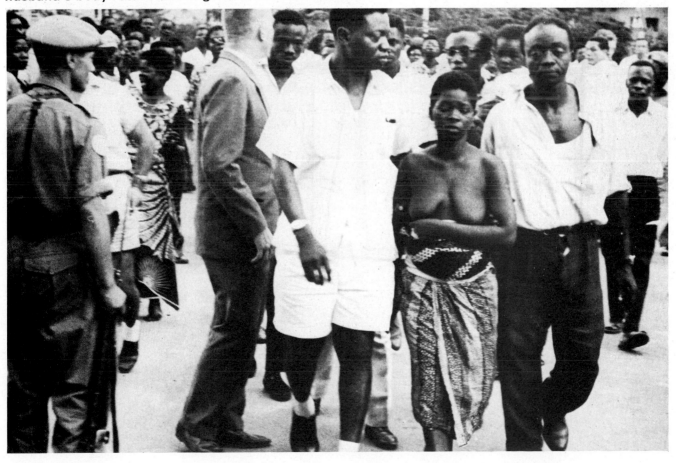

RAFAEL TRUJILLO

Born October 24, 1891   San Cristobal, Dominican Republic
Died May 30, 1961   Santo Domingo, Dominican Republic

Dictator of the Dominican Republic from 1930 until he was assassinated in 1961

Assassination conspirators include:
General Román Fernández, secretary of state for the Armed Forces
Brigadier General Juan Tomas Díaz
Luis Amiama Tío, businessman
Lieutenant Amado García Guerrero, aide-de-camp
Roberto Pastoriza, civil engineer
Pedro Livio Cedeño, businessman
General Antonio Imbert
Salvador Estrella
Huascar Antonia Tejeda Pimentel
Antonio de la Muza Vasquez

For over thirty years the Dominican Republic was ruled by Rafael Trujillo. The "Era of Trujillo", as the period from 1930 to 1961 has come to be called, was marked by military force and political repression. By 1961 only one twentieth century dictator—Salazar of Portugal—could claim to have held power for a longer period of time. Not only was Trujillo absolute ruler of the island republic, the Generalissimo and his family owned much of the island's wealth.

Rafael Leonidas Trujillo Molina was born in 1891 in the town of San Cristobal, about twenty miles from the capital city of Santo Domingo. He came from a large and financially modest family—his father worked in the town post office. According to one version of his early life—dictators are wont to retouch their personal histories—after elementary school he worked as a telegraph operator. According to a very different version he worked as an informer and procurer of women for the U.S. soldiers stationed in the Dominican Republic.

He then enlisted as a second lieutenant in the Dominican National Guard. Fortunately for his career, the United States was holding the Dominican Republic under military occupation from 1916 to 1924 in order to protect loans and investments. His military skills caught the attention of a U.S. Marine Corp officer, and it was arranged for Trujillo to take a brief course at a Marine-operated training camp. Under Marine Corp sponsorship, Trujillo rose rapidly in the Dominican Army. By the time the last U.S. troops left in 1924 he was a brigadier general and chief of staff of the Dominican Army.

Early in 1930 the Dominican Republic experienced its thirtieth revolution in modern times, and Trujillo threw in his lot with the rebels. Afterward he announced himself a candidate for the presidency. He easily won an overwhelming election victory; there were no opposing candidates. In his inaugural speech Trujillo promised that his administration would be dedicated to "democracy and public welfare". Eighteen days later a hurricane swept through the country killing thousands and leveling all but four hundred houses in the capital city. He promptly declared martial law and deployed troops to maintain order. For the next thirty years his iron grip upon the country was not loosened. He spread terror throughout the land with his strong-arm squad—called the "AR 42" after the 42nd Company of U.S. Marines.

Even though Trujillo had gained control of a nearly bankrupt government, he restored the nation's credit and repaid the national debt twenty years before it was due. This was accomplished by imposing a completely repressive, near confiscatory taxing policy on the people. By 1959 the Dominican Republic was one of the few countries free of external debt.

Trujillo launched a vast program of school construction, and in thirty years he claimed that the illiteracy rate dropped from seventy percent to four percent. Pure drinking water and modern hospitals and clinics were provided. The excellent new roads had military check points every few miles. Dominican cities became world-renowned for their immaculate streets.

All the improvements, however, were made at a great cost. Some estimate that as many as one thousand of his political opponents were slaughtered in the first year of his rule. The anti-Trujillo exile community grew month by month, and the Dominican Republic soon became known for the bizarre deaths of Trujillo's victims. In many cases people would be arrested with no charges placed against them—within a short time announcements would be made that the prisoners had been "killed while trying to escape". Enemies of the Trujillo family were especially prone to "suicides" and mysterious auto accidents occurred at an alarming rate. Such accidents often involved opponents' wives and relatives; usually the accidents happened along the cliff-hugging coastal roads. If the family was wealthy, the chauffeur had to die also in order to add a note of authenticity. It is little wonder that Trujillo, his secret police and not so secret army were feared by all strata of society.

Trujillo received unwanted worldwide prominence in 1937 when reports leaked out concerning the wholesale massacre of Haitian squatters. For some years black workers from Haiti (which shares the island with the Dominican Republic) had come to harvest sugarcane. It was the tradition that the Haitians would return home after the harvest, but in 1937 they wanted to remain. Allegedly at Trujillo's orders the army killed an estimated 12,000 to 15,000 men, women, and children within thirty-six hours. The dictator never effectively denied the slaughter, referring to it as a purely "local affair".

Throughout his long rule Trujillo held the designation Chief of State, but from time to time he allowed either one of his brothers or some other hand-picked lieutenant to be the president, at least in name. He himself held numerous titles: Benefactor of the Fatherland, Liberator, His Illustrious Superiority, Rebuilder of Financial Independence of the Republic, Father of the New Fatherland, Chief Protector of the Dominican Working Class, Genius of Peace, and his favorite one, *El Jefe* (The Chief).

Trujillo's secret police were infamous for their skill at keeping an eye on Dominicans at home and overseas. Despite his repressive methods, until the late 1940s, the dictator was tolerant of Communists and other left-wing elements, even welcoming Republican refugees at the end of the Spanish Civil War. One of these refugees was Jesus de Galindez, a Basque scholar who was given a government job and served for a time as tutor for Trujillo's children. After a few years Galindez became disillusioned and went to the U.S. where he began to work on a book critical of the dictator. He claimed knowledge of 140 political assassinations and openly criticized the spy network. On March 12, 1956, Dr. Galindez left

his work as an instructor at Columbia University, entered a subway station and was never seen again. An American pilot for the Dominican airline claimed to have flown the kidnapped Galindez to the Dominican Republic. The pilot soon vanished as did a close friend of his.

Naturally the dictator had to be lavish in fees and retainers to his lobbyists and men in Washington who did what they could to improve this gruesome image. At one time he retained the services of Franklin Delano Roosevelt, Jr.; at another time he invited to the island the whole U.S. House Agriculture Committee. He won the support of Senators James Eastland and Allen Ellender as well as that of Congressman Harold Cooley. Congressional support helped to ensure a good share of the lucrative sugar quota. To remind the Dominican Republic's citizenry of his beneficence, thousands of Trujillo statues dotted the cities and countryside. The capital city was renamed Ciudad Trujillo. Soon there were Trujillo mountains, Trujillo highways and Trujillo parks. Motorists dared not mock the roadside billboards that proclaimed "Thank you, Trujillo". Neon signs flashed the message "Trujillo and God."

It will come as no surprise to learn that the Trujillo family amassed a huge fortune, since among other fees the Benefactor received a percentage share of all public works contracts. He also owned the monopolies on salt, cigarettes, lumber, matches and peanut oil. When his son Rafael, Jr. purchased a Mercedes-Benz for Kim Novak and another for Zsa Zsa Gabor, it made no dent in the family budget. At all of his twelve lavishly furnished ranches and villas a full set of servants prepared elaborate meals for him—one never knew when *El Jefe* might drop by for dinner. Of course each mansion also contained a complete wardrobe for the dictator.

By 1960 Trujillo had built up three decades of legitimate resentment in the hearts of his enemies, many of whom held prominent positions in the government. Numerous exile groups competed with each other in denouncing Trujillo, and more important, Trujillo began to alienate the United States. Beginning about 1947, Trujillo became increasingly anti-Communist, a trend that had peaked in 1959 when a Cuban-led invasion attempt was thwarted. But by 1960 his attacks on Castro and Cuba became less vociferous. At the time that the United States government began to support dissidents who were planning Trujillo's assassination, Trujillo's policies became more pro-Communist.

In January of 1960 Trujillo crushed a planned coup against him. Mass arrests were made and whole groups were convicted and sentenced to as long as thirty years in prison. Even relatives of the dictator's friend Brigadier General Juan Tomas Díaz were implicated. This attempted coup had three important results. First of all, the Catholic hierarchy which had been favorably disposed to the regime for a few years after a Papal Concord in 1954, issued a pastoral letter signed by the country's bishops, urging the dictator to abandon his repressions against the people. Second, Díaz was forced into retirement, and third, many of the conspirators became convinced that assassination was the only means of removing the dictator from power.

The plotters were mainly recruited from among professional and middle-class persons. They drew up plans for the establishment of a junta for the time when Trujillo would no longer be in control. Apparently the group consisted of some top government officials and even people close to Trujillo. For example, General Román Fernández, who was the secretary of state for the Armed Forces, was married to one of Trujillo's nieces. Retired Brigadier General Juan Tomas Díaz was ostensibly a close friend of the Benefactor before his forced retirement. Luis Amiama Tío was a wealthy businessman. The following were directly involved in the murder: Lieutenant Amado García Guerrero, an aide-de-camp; Roberto Pastoriza, a civilian engineer; Pedro Livio Cedeño, administrator of the Hercules Battery Manufacturing Company who had been a close associate of the dictator, having served as military commandant in various provinces until he retired from the army; Antonio Imbert, a general; Salvador Estrella, whose father was an army officer; and two others, Huascar Antonia Tejeda Pimentel and Antonio de la Muza Vasquez.

Relations between the Catholic hierarchy and the dictator grew steadily worse. *El Jefe* was angered when the bishops rejected a request that the title "Benefactor of the Church" be conferred upon him. However, Trujillo's biggest blunder was his alleged instigation of an attempt on the life of President Romulo Betancourt of Venezuela on June 24, 1960. The charges were brought before the Organization of American States, and diplomatic relations were broken off between most member states and the Dominican Republic. There was a partial interruption of economic relations with the immediate suspension of all trade in arms. In August the United States broke off diplomatic relations, and in January of 1961 the OAS recommended that shipments of oil products, trucks and truck parts be stopped.

Trujillo's reaction to all this was to take a more pro-Communist line. His official radio station, Radio Caribe, began carrying the news reports of Tass, the Soviet news agency. He allowed leftists to take over a newspaper. He sent representatives of his government to some of the Communist nations, and he promised to let a Fidelista political party organize. These diplomatic moves were either attempts to pressure the U.S. into relenting in its anti-Trujillo policies, or else they were serious maneuvers designed to prevent Trujillo from being completely isolated. A third possibility is that *El Jefe* simply took these actions to spite the Dominican Republic's upper class for which he had a lifelong hatred.

According to the U.S. Senate Intelligence Committee report of 1975, from early 1960 and continuing to the time of the assassination, the United States government generally supported the dissidents who were planning the assassination. Some U.S. government personnel were aware that the dissidents planned to kill Trujillo. American officials furnished pistols and carbines but refused a request for machine guns. The United States consul in the Dominican Republic served as the American contact with the dissident groups plotting the overthrow of the Dominican Republic's dictator. The Senate Committee found conflicting evidence as to whether the weapons were knowingly supplied for use in the assassination and whether any of the American-supplied guns were present at the scene of the murder. Let us examine more closely the role of the U.S. government in the Trujillo assassination.

The United States government did not initiate the plot. Rather, U.S. officials responded to requests for aid from local dissidents whose aim was clearly to kill Trujillo. American officials clearly desired the overthrow of Trujillo, and it was widely known that the dissidents intended to kill him.

On February 15, 1961, Secretary of State Dean Rusk prepared a memo for the president, and Richard Bissell of the CIA did the same on February 17. Although both the State Department and the CIA had information concerning the plans to kill Trujillo if possible, neither memo mentioned such a contingency. Instead, Bissell's February 17 memo to Kennedy mentioned the fact that the dissident leaders had notified the CIA of "their plan of action which they felt could be implemented if they were provided with arms for three hundred men, explosives and remote control detonation devices." The memo to Kennedy did not mention to what use these explosives might be put. Actually the dissidents' favorite plan for eliminating Trujillo was to blow him to bits by means of a bomb detonated by remote control.

Whether Trujillo by this time had got wind of these plans is not known. However there were apparently authoritative reports that the dictator, starting in 1960, had been busy shipping part of his huge fortune (estimated at between $800,000,000 and $1 billion) to Switzerland and Liechtenstein.

On March 31, 1961, the passage of carbines to the plotters was approved by CIA headquarters. The State Department's representative in the Dominican Republic agreed to pass the carbines, but he was requested not to communicate this information to the State Department officials in Washington. Thus neither the State Department nor the White House knew about the passage of weapons for several weeks. Also no disclosure was made outside the CIA, except to the State Department representative in the Dominican Republic, of the fact that weapons had been sent to the Dominican Republic via diplomatic pouch. After the April 17 failure of the Cuban Bay of Pigs adventure, CIA headquarters requested their operatives in the Dominican Republic to tell the dissidents to "turn off" the assassination attempt, because the U.S. was not prepared to "cope with the aftermath". The dissidents replied that the assassination was their own business and that it could not be aborted to suit the convenience of the U.S. government.

When did Kennedy learn that the plan to overthrow the Trujillo regime would include the assassination of Trujillo? According to the Senate Intelligence Committee report, by early May of 1961 senior American officials, including President Kennedy, knew that the dissidents intended to kill Trujillo. The White House, State Department and CIA all knew that the U.S. had provided the dissidents with rifles and pistols.

On May 16 President Kennedy approved National Security Council recommendations that the U.S. should not initiate the overthrow of Trujillo until it was known what kind of regime would succeed the dictator. This was consistent with the CIA's attempts to discourage the planned assassination. After deciding to discourage the conspirators, the Director of Central Intelligence ordered that machine guns be not passed along to the plotters. On May 30—the night before the murder—Kennedy cabled the State Department representative in the Dominican Republic that the U.S. "as [a] matter of general policy cannot condone assassination." However, the cable also stated that if the plotters succeeded in assassinating Trujillo, and thereby established a provisional government, the U.S. would recognize and support them. One interpretation of the telegram is that it was designed to avoid a charge that the U.S. shared responsibility for the assassination.

The conspirators, meanwhile, had planned well. After three months' observation, they had discovered that not only did Trujillo visit his widowed mother every night but also that on the nights he planned to drive out to his farm after visiting his mother, he would put on his uniform. What they were waiting for was an evening when he would take the fifteen-mile highway to his farm—for it was along that route that they considered he could be easily ambushed. Amado García, who served as an aide-de-camp at the national palace in Ciudad Trujillo, was to pass the word to his fellow conspirators when Trujillo planned to visit his farm, Estancia Fundacion, in his home town of San Cristobal. On the evening of May 30, 1961, Trujillo was seen dressed in his uniform—the signal that he planned to visit his farm (and allegedly one of his mistresses). The alert went out. Two cars stationed themselves at the outskirts of Ciudad Trujillo along the main road to San Cristobal while another was to follow the Generalissimo's car from the palace.

As Trujillo's turquoise blue and gray sedan passed the parked cars, they pulled out to follow. After several miles the murder car came from behind with its lights out; it pulled alongside and began firing rounds of ammunition into Trujillo's car. According to the chauffer's account, the Generalissimo shouted, "I am wounded. Let us stop and fight". Then Trujillo began firing his revolver while the chauffeur fired two machine guns in succession. When the firing stopped, Trujillo was dead, his car riddled with over fifty bullet holes and the seats stained with blood. The assassins pounded Trujillo's body, causing facial contusions and practically destroying his left arm, before dumping the body in the trunk of one of the cars and then driving it back to the city. There the assassins parked the car in a garage and attempted to make their escape.

Unfortunately for the assassins, one of Trujillo's lieutenants happened to be at a restaurant very near the site of the ambush that night. He heard the gunfire and, after making a preliminary investigation, immediately alerted the police and armed forces. The chauffeur, who evidently had been left for dead, was able to identify one of the conspirators, García, by his voice during the gun battle. In addition, Pedro Cedeño, a conspirator who was taken to a hospital after being badly wounded, was turned over to police and implicated some of his fellow conspirators. Eventually all the assassins were captured and ultimately executed, except for Luis Amiama Tío and General Antonio Imbert who escaped. They both later returned to assume high positions in their country after the trouble had died down.

Trujillo's son, Rafael, Jr., together with President Joaquin Balaguer, whom Trujillo had placed in the office, attempted to maintain stability and fill the political void left by the Benefactor. Young Rafael, however, was more known for his playboy habits and extravagant tastes and seemed more concerned with maintaining his family's station than assuming his father's political leadership. The weakened regime did attempt to grant the opposition an orderly political process for change, and elections were planned for 1962. However, Trujillo's two brothers, Hector and Jose Arisemende (known as "the wicked uncles"), without the knowledge or consent of Rafael, Jr. and Balaguer, attempted to subvert the democratic process by staging an unsuccessful coup attempt that served only to inspire a threat of U.S. intervention and eventually lead to the whole Trujillo family's self-exile. As strong a political machine as Trujillo had created, it had little life beyond his own□

Above: Wearing the uniform of
Generalissimo, President Rafael Trujillo
takes the oath of office to continue as
president for another five-year term,
August 16, 1947

Below: August 16, 1957, Generalissimo Rafael
Trujillo (saluting) at the inauguration of his
brother, Hector B. Trujillo, to a second term
as president of the Dominican Republic; Dona
Maria Martinez de Trujillo, the Generalissimo's
wife, and his granddaughter are beside him

Rafael Trujillo, Jr. with actress Kim Novak, after reportedly giving her a Mercedes-Benz

Opposite: The Generalissimo with his son, Rafael, Jr., at an international polo series, April 1953

Film star Zsa Zsa Gabor poses beside her new $5,600 190SL Mercedes-Benz, a gift from Rafael, Jr.

Above: Trujillo (straw hat in hand) reviews U.S. Marines upon his arrival at Union Station in Washington, D.C.

Below: Trujillo (R) and U.S. Secretary of State Cordell Hull sign a treaty ending control of the Dominican Republic's customs service, September 24, 1940

Francis Cardinal Spellman (L), archbishop of New York, is shown with Trujillo at the opening of the International Catholic Cultural Congress for World Peace in Ciudad Trujillo

The Chevrolet sedan in which Trujillo was riding when he was assassinated; bloodstained seats and over fifty bullet holes attest to the fierce gun battle

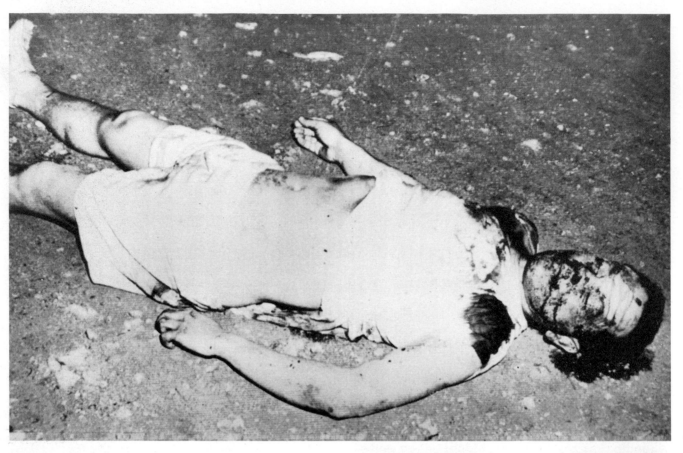

Above: The body of Lieutenant Amado García Guerrero, one of the chief conspirators, is shown after Guerrero was killed by police as he reportedly resisted arrest, June 2, 1961

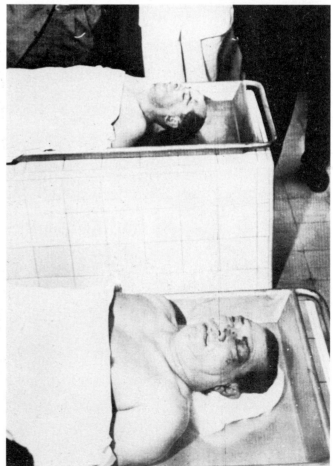

The bodies of two of the conspirators, Antonio de la Muza Vasquez (rear) and Juan Tomas Díaz

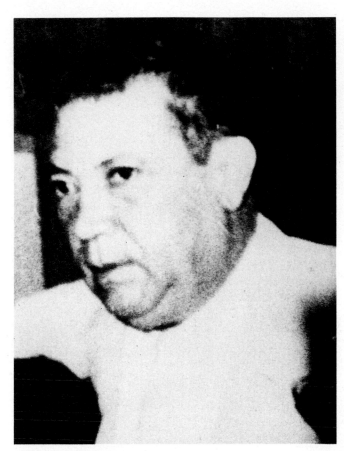

Retired Brigadier General Juan Tomas Díaz

Captain Zacarias de la Cruz, Trujillo's chauffeur, who was left for dead by the assassins

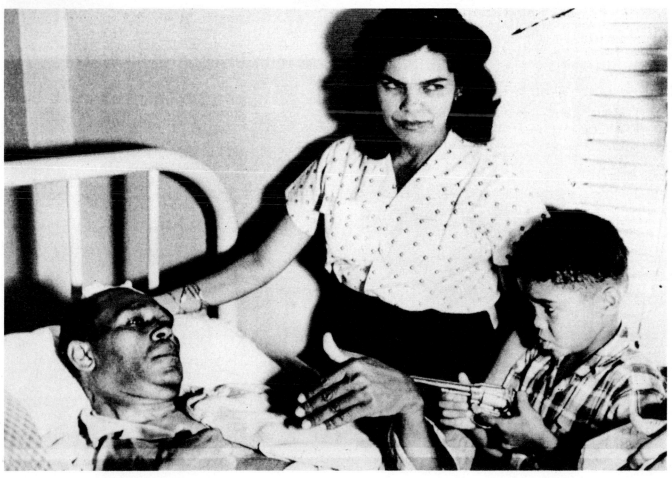

Flor de Oro Trujillo, 42-year-old daughter of Rafael Trujillo, former wife of playboy race car driver Porfirio Rubirosa, en route home for her father's funeral

Funeral services for Trujillo were held in churches all over the Dominican Republic. The family attended burial services at the church in San Cristobal where the body was laid to rest under the altar

Not all Dominicans mourned the death of the Benefactor. The coup de grâce is delivered here to a huge bust of Trujillo

NGO DINH DIEM

Born 1901   near Hue, Vietnam
Died November 2, 1963   Saigon, South Vietnam

A civil servant, he entered politics at an early age and became minister of the interior; dropping out of politics, he then left the country for a number of years returning as prime minister in 1954; elected president in 1955, he led a repressive regime dependent on U.S. support until his assassination in 1963

Alleged assassin:
A Vietnamese tank corps major, whose name was never released

According to the U.S. Senate Intelligence Committee report released on November 20, 1975, the United States directly supported the coup that overthrew the government of President Ngo Dinh Diem in 1963. However, that study also states that there is no evidence that American officials favored the assassination of Diem. Rather the murder was a "spontaneous act which occurred during the coup and was carried out without United States involvement or support." The so-called Pentagon Papers published in 1971 give a detailed account of U.S. involvement and support of the November coup.

The background to the assassination of Diem and his brother Ngo Dinh Nhu is a complex one of coup and counter-coup plots. Diem, the bachelor president, had fallen more and more under the sway of his mystical and tyrannical brother Nhu and Nhu's wife. The family came to use more and more repressive measures during its last year in power; no doubt these actions triggered the coup that finally overthrew them.

Diem was born near Hue in 1901. He was a Roman Catholic who began the novitiate for the priesthood when he was 15 years old but soon dropped out to attend a school for civil servants. After graduating with highest honors he served in a number of posts as district and then province chief. At the age of 32 he was named minister of the interior but resigned, protesting that the real power was exercised by French colonial officials. During World War II he refused to become premier and when the war ended, the Communists held him prisoner for six months after he rejected their offers of a ministerial post. In 1950 he left Vietnam and traveled to Japan, Europe and the United States. He lived for a while at Maryknoll Seminary in Lakewood, New Jersey and in a Belgian monastery.

In 1954 Diem returned to Vietnam as prime minister and in 1955 was elected president. For the next eight years he consolidated his power and became increasingly dependent upon the advice of his brother and sixter-in-law, the Nhus, who played upon his not inconsiderable vanity and his apparently justifiable suspicion of others. By 1963, however, Nhu had become isolated from reality. He refused to listen to facts that contradicted his preconceptions and spent much of his time playing one group off against another. Nhu had his own private army, the Vietnamese Special Forces; Madame Nhu had her own female auxiliary corps, and the couple vied with each other in intrigue. Diem also listened to the advice of his other brother Archbishop Ngo Dinh Thuc, a dominant figure in central Vietnam.

The sparks that led to the November coup were set off by a religious and political controversy between Buddhist and Catholic Vietnamese. When Vietnam had been divided in 1954 into a Communist north and an anti-Communist south, over a half a million Catholics fled from the north into the south where they became strong supporters of the Diem regime. Buddhists claimed that Catholics received the better government jobs and the allocation of the best lands and that Catholic villages benefited most from the government's relief and aid programs, agricultural loans and land grants for schools and hospitals.

The Buddhist protests against the Diem policies broke into open conflict in May of 1963 in Hue; nine worshipers were shot and killed by government troops. The controversy centered around the right of the Buddhists to display religious flags to commemorate the 2,507th anniversary of the Buddha's birth, a celebration that coincided with one commemorating the 25th anniversary of Ngo Dinh Thuc's consecration as archbishop. When the leader of the Buddhists in central Vietnam refused to send Thuc a congratulatory telegram, the government began to enforce against the Buddhists a two-year-old ban against religious flags, even though Catholics had been allowed to fly the Vatican flag during Thuc's celebration. The Buddhists defiantly displayed their flags and the government backed down. At this point the Buddhists proceeded with their long-planned May 8 mass demonstration against religious persecution which was smashed by government troops. Incidents continued including the widely-publicized sacrificial suicides by fire that were reported around the world, creating a worldwide revulsion against Diem. The United States attempted to get Diem to solve the problem quietly, but Nhu and his wife brought undocumented charges that the Buddhists were Communist-inspired. Madame Nhu referred to the self-immolations as Buddhist "barbecues".

By July 10, 1963, a U.S. Special Intelligence Estimate reported that "if—as is likely—Diem fails to carry out truly and promptly the commitments he has made to the Buddhists, disorders will probably flare again and the chances of a coup or assassination attempts against him will become better than ever ... a non-Communist successor regime ... given continued support from the U.S. could provide reasonably effective leadership for the government and the war effort. ..." The CIA had been tipped off about two developing coup attempts. On August 21, in an action that contributed to his undoing, Nhu ordered a drastic night-time attack by Special Forces troops on Buddhist pagodas. One thousand four hundred people were arrested, most of them monks. Many were beaten and imprisoned. American officials were particularly angry because the Vietnamese Special Forces had been financed and trained by the CIA for covert war operations when, in fact, they were being used as if they were Nhu's private army. In addition, during the raids, Nhu had the telephone lines to the American Embassy cut and had sought to give the Americans the impression that the attacks were conducted by regular army forces.

Two days later the army generals conspiring against Diem first sought official American support. On August 24 the U.S. State Department sent a message to Henry Cabot Lodge, the new American ambassador in Saigon, to the effect that the United States could no longer tolerate the powerful role of Nhu and his wife. "We wish [to] give Diem reasonable opportunity to remove [the] Nhus, but if he remains obdurate, then we are prepared to accept the obvious implication that we can no longer support Diem. You may also tell appropriate military commanders we will give them direct support in any interim period of breakdown [of] central government mechanism." Lodge suggested that "we go straight to the generals with our demands, without informing Diem. Would tell them [that] we [are] prepared [to] have Diem without [the] Nhus but it is in effect up to them whether we keep him." This suggestion was agreed to by Washington. The conspirators were informed by the CIA that "we cannot be of any help during initial action of assuming power of state. Entirely their own action, win or lose. Don't expect to be bailed out." The plotters were informed that the U.S. "hoped bloodshed can be avoided or reduced to absolute minimum."

The plotters seem to have been composed of two separate groups: one group was composed of leading generals, the other of younger officers in alliance with workers and students. Nhu had not expected the violent student unrest that had taken place after the pagoda attacks. Schools and colleges had to be closed and thousands of students arrested. During September and October the CIA offered to "assist in tactical planning" of the coup and provided the conspirators with sensitive information including plans and armament inventories of the secret installation of the Vietnamese Special Forces. There was a bitter division among Americans in Saigon. Ambassador Lodge was in favor of a coup, General Paul Harkins, head of the U.S. military advisory group, opposed it.

United States officials encouraged the generals in their coup plans by cutting off some economic aid deliveries to the Diem regime. Madame Nhu, who was in the U.S. at this time ostensibly to gain support for her brother-in-law's regime, drew a great deal of press coverage as she, accompanied by her daughter, spoke out against the cuts in U.S. aid to South Vietnam.

While the coup was being planned Diem and Nhu attempted to counter growing U.S. pressure by opening up contacts with Hanoi for a negotiated settlement of the war. After DeGaulle, President of France, had made a statement implying that an agreement between North and South Vietnam was possible and that France would support a neutral Vietnam, Nhu opened up contacts with Roger Lalouette, the French ambassador in Saigon, and Mieczylaw Maneli, member of the Polish delegation of the International Control Commission. It may be that at first these steps toward an agreement with the Communists were meant simply to put pressure on the United States to continue its support for Diem and the Nhus, but it is generally conceded that within a short time Nhu, at least, was convinced that he might make a deal with the Communists.

In any event, in October Nhu formulated a fantastic plan that probably sealed his doom—he planned an elaborate fake coup to be staged in Saigon. According to this bizarre scheme troops loyal to him would stage a counterfeit coup with enough bloodshed and killing of American civilians to be convincing. Diem and Nhu were to "escape" to a seaside resort town and then return to "re-conquer" Saigon. This was supposed to show the Americans that they had a genuine dependency on the Diem regime to maintain essential stability. Unfortunately for Diem and Nhu, the leader in this fake coup was also in on the real coup!

At 1:30 P.M. November 1, 1963, the revolt began with the CIA agent, who was the contact man between the generals and Ambassador Lodge, stationed in the rebel command post. The junior officers, who previously had been plotting independently from the generals, worked in smooth coordination with the leading dissidents. In less than an hour the central police headquarters, the post office and the radio station were captured. From the beginning Diem and Nhu had been duped into assuming that the coup about which they were being informed was the fake coup. When it finally dawned upon them that they had been tricked, they frantically attempted to telephone various regional and provisional headquarters for aid but to no avail.

At about 8:00 P.M. Diem and Nhu sneaked out of the palace through a special tunnel and were driven, concealed in a Red Cross ambulance, to the large house of a rich Chinese friend in Cholon, the Chinese section of Saigon. When the palace came under attack at about 3:45 A.M., most of its defenders did not realize that Diem and Nhu had already escaped. Direct telephone communications between the house in Cholon and the palace had previously been set up for just such contingencies, so Diem's military aide in the palace relayed to Diem details of the attack on the palace.

When the palace surrendered at about 6:00 A.M. one of Nhu's officers revealed where the hideout was. When a military officer reached the house in Cholon he immediately used a telephone to call the palace and tell the rebel leaders his whereabouts. Diem and Nhu, listening in on an extension, realized by the strange voice that they were in immediate danger and fled to a nearby Catholic church. Around 9:00 A.M. Diem got to a telephone, called one of the generals leading the coup and agreed to surrender. Armored personnel carriers were sent to pick them up.

The general in charge of bringing back the prisoners rode in one of the carriers and the prisoners in the other. A major who had a grudge against Nhu for having ordered the execution of one of his close friends accompanied the prisoners. An eyewitness report described the assassination which the generals at first called suicide, then "accidental suicide". Diem and Nhu sat with their hands tied behind their backs. While Diem remained silent, Nhu and the major began to trade insults. Suddenly the major lunged at Nhu with his bayonet and stabbed him fifteen or twenty times. Then he took out his revolver and shot Diem in the back of the head; seeing Nhu's body still twitching on the floor, the major administered the *coup de grâce* by putting a bullet through Nhu's head also.

The murder of Diem led to an even greater U.S. commitment to the war in Vietnam; soon afterward the dramatic escalation of U.S. involvement began and the great tragedy of the all-consuming war began to unfold□

Ngo Dinh Nhu, the brother and chief political adviser of President Diem, 1957

Above: Admiral Arthur W. Radford (R), chairman of the U.S. Joint Chiefs of Staff, meeting with President Ngo Dinh Diem in 1956

Below: Concerned with the spread of Communist influence in Indochina, President Kennedy's special military adviser, General Maxwell Taylor (L) meets with Diem during a fact-finding trip

Above: A young Buddhist monk burns himself to death in Saigon's Market Square, October 1963, in protest at the Diem Administration's religions policies. Diem lost considerable support in the U.S. as a result of these deaths by self-immolation

Below left: Ngo Dinh Le Thuy, Nhu's daughter, as a member of the Vietnamese Para-Military Women's Corps, training to bear arms against the Viet Cong

Below: Madame Nhu and her daughter arrive in Rome in September 1963 as part of a global tour to lobby for support for her brother-in-law, Diem, and his regime

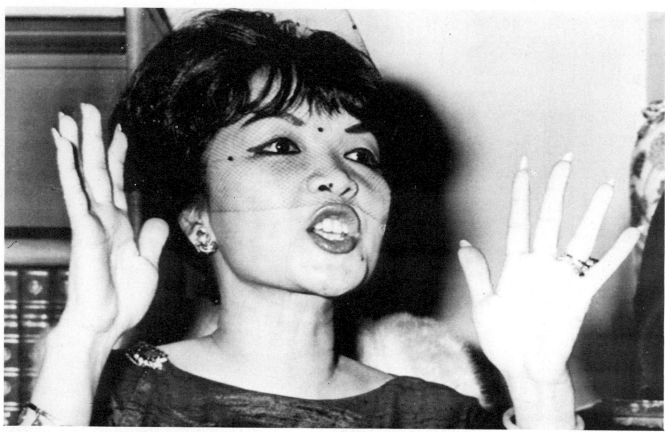

Above: Madame Nhu, nicknamed the "Dragon Lady", at one of the numerous press conferences she held while visiting the West

Below: The bodies of Diem (R) and his brother Ngo Dinh Nhu, disguised as priests, lie in an armored personnel carrier November 2, shortly after being assassinated during a military coup

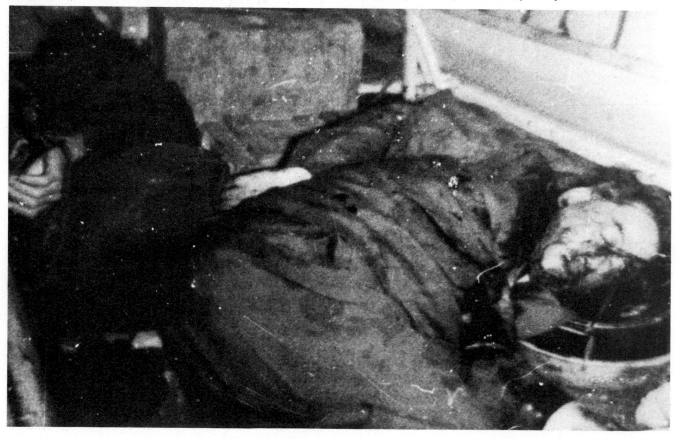

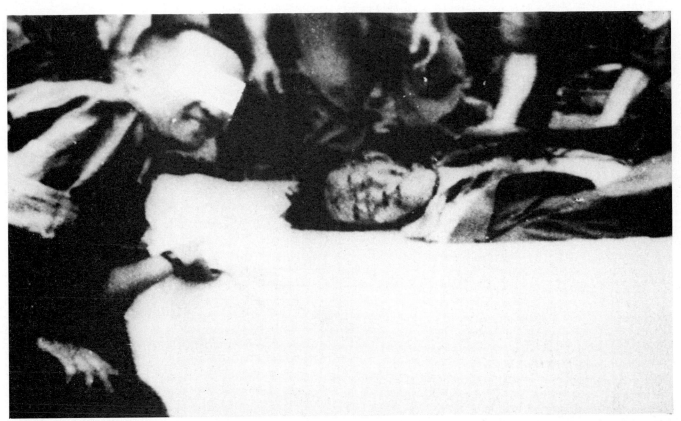

Above: A smiling Vietnamese Army officer, his face partially blocked out, is pictured helping to lift the body of Nhu from the personnel carrier in which he and his brother Diem were assassinated

Below: The body of another brother of Diem's, Ngo Dinh Can, is cut down from a pole after Can was executed in Saigon, May 9, 1964

Madame Nhu, on the NBC "Tomorrow" show, May 7, 1975, said that the Communists' control of Saigon "cannot last long"

JOHN
FITZGERALD KENNEDY

Born May 29, 1917 Brookline, Massachusetts
Died November 22, 1963 Dallas, Texas

Thirty-fifth president of the United States

Alleged sole assassin:
Lee Harvey Oswald, 24-year-old ex-Marine

President John Fitzgerald Kennedy was shot to death at 12:30 P.M., November 22, 1963, while he and his wife, accompanied by Texas Governor and Mrs. John B. Connally, were driving in a motorcade through downtown Dallas, Texas. The assassination of the young thirty-fifth president of the United States was an outrage that shocked the world.

A number of people personally close to the president as well as several important political figures had misgivings about the trip and warned Kennedy not to make what amounted to a politically expedient visit to Texas, a state that was potentially antagonistic towards him. The Secret Service, given the huge responsibility of checking out the presidential route while in Texas, were apprehensive as well. Kennedy liked to shake hands, disliked riding in bubble-top cars and was a hard man to protect. But politics was the name of the game and John Kennedy was above all a tough politician. He decided that, regardless of any real or imagined undercurrents of discontent among the people of Texas toward him, it was important at that time for him, accompanied by Mrs. Kennedy, to make the trip.

A surprisingly receptive crowd met the presidential plane at Dallas's Love Field, craning their necks to see the good-looking president and his stylish first lady. A full scale motorcade had been arranged to bring the president's party into Dallas to the World Trade Center where Kennedy was to speak. According to the Secret Service, they had planned to position the cars so that the president's Lincoln Continental would be seventh in line, but for some still obscure reason the president's limousine ended up second in line, immediately behind the lead car carrying local officials and Dallas Police Chief Jesse Curry. The car carrying the Secret Service agents followed. Normally the press ride in the car directly preceding the president to allow for better photo coverage, but today this car was fourteenth in line, bringing up the very rear of the motorcade.

Entering Dealey Plaza, the motorcade had turned off Houston Street and was proceeding down Elm Street where the Texas School Book Depository Building is located, when three shots rang out, mortally wounding the president and injuring Governor Connally. Upon realizing what had happened, the driver of the lead car and the driver of the Lincoln limousine quickly accellerated as Secret Service agent Clinton J. Hill climbed onto the back of the Lincoln and pushed Mrs. Kennedy, who had crawled up on the trunk, back down and out of danger. The motorcade sped off to the Parkland Hospital where Kennedy was pronounced dead.

The official findings of the Warren Commission (the President's Commission on the Assassination of President Kennedy) identified the assassin as one Lee Harvey Oswald who fired the fatal shots from a sixth-floor window of the Texas School Book Depository Building where he was employed as a $1.25 an hour stock boy.

The Commission based its entire report on the "single assassin theory" that Lee Harvey Oswald acted alone and was in no way connected with an assassination conspiracy. The Commission found that Oswald fired a 6.5 mm bolt-action, clip-fed 1938 Mannlicher-Carcano rifle from a sixth-floor stock room of the Texas School Book Depository Building, where the gun was subsequently found and proven to belong to Oswald. Three shots were fired by Oswald. The first shot entered Kennedy's back five and a half inches below his collar line, leaving via his throat, striking Connally in the back, exiting from his side, entering and leaving his upheld wrist and finally lodging in his left thigh. The second shot went wide, striking the curb directly at the feet of a bystander, James T. Tague. The third and fatal shot struck Kennedy in the head, shattering parts of brain and skull away from his head.

Assuming, as the Commission's report did, that Oswald's rifle was the only gun fired at Dealey Plaza, only three shots could have been fired from it in the 5.6 seconds that elapsed from the point Kennedy sustained the first shot until the last obviously fatal shot to the head. Having accounted for the effect of the last two bullets, one to the curb, one to the head, this leaves only one bullet, the first, to have caused no less than seven wounds in both Kennedy and Connally, based on the Commission findings.

Witnesses agree that a bullet did go astray and that the last shot struck the president in the head, but there is much dispute among witnesses concerning the direction from which the last bullet came. Conclusions about the assassination depend on the reliability of different types of evidence.

Relying on geometrics to test out the course of the first bullet: From the sixth-floor window, the bullet had to have been traveling in a downward direction. Entering the president's body at a point five and a half inches below the collar line, the bullet was presumed by the Commission to have exited through the neck leaving a small slit which was the only other wound on the body besides the entry wound in the back and the fatal head wound. Since this bullet was known not to have struck any bone in the president's body, which could have deflected its downward direction, it is difficult to accept the Commission's finding that it exited in an upward direction through the throat.

Relying on the time element to test out the one man, one gun theory: The famous Zapruder film, the basis for much analysis regarding the shooting, shows ten frames elapsing between the last point at which Kennedy could have been struck and when Connally was first hit, or just over one half of a second elapsing between the two impacts. According to expert testimony, the bullet had to have been traveling at a speed of approximately 1,775 feet per second. In order for the same bullet which hit Kennedy to have then struck Connally, sitting only a few feet in front in the limousine, that bullet would have had to have been suspended in mid air. Also it is impossible for the Oswald rifle to have been fired twice within the just over half second time lapse, as expert riflemen needed 2.3 seconds to fire it twice.

Relying on the element of motion: Laws of motion dictate that an object when struck will move in the same direction as the object striking it. A bullet fired from Oswald's position would have, on impact, forced the head in a forward direction. The Zapruder film shows Kennedy's head flung backwards after the impact of the fatal bullet to his head.

Lee Harvey Oswald was born October 18, 1939, in New Orleans. He was killed by Jack Ruby, a strip joint owner, two days after the assassination while being held in the custody of police authorities. According to the Commission's portrayal and selective evidence describing Oswald, he appeared to be a Marxist who had no particular loyalty to his country. However, if one fills out the story, it becomes inconsistant with the official portrayal.

Oswald entered the Marine Corps at the age of 17 and received a hardship discharge in 1959 due to illness in the family. Almost immediately after arriving home, he made a trip to the Soviet Union (on a luxury liner for an amount neither he nor his family could have possibly afforded) where he offered to give to the Soviets trategic information he had obtained while in the Marines. (During this time the FBI ran a check on Oswald, and in spite of these activities, the CIA and U.S. embassy in Moscow notified back that his record was good.) After two and a half years Oswald returned to the U.S., his hardship discharge having since been changed to a dishonorable discharge, with his Russian bride, Marina, the daughter of a KGB officer. With a U.S. State Department loan he and his wife moved to New Orleans. (Here he applied for a U.S. citizen's passport and received one in less than twenty-four hours—an unusual occurrence considering his activities in the Soviet Union and the fact that passport processing, alone, generally takes a good deal longer than one day unless motivated by some special circumstance.)

In New Orleans, Oswald became a member of the Fair Play for Cuba Committee whose offices oddly were shared with a group having CIA connections involved in planning the second invasion in Cuba. Oswald made a number of contacts with different CIA officials during this time, and in fact in Mexico City in 1963, he was met by two

CIA agents sent there to see him by their superior E. Howard Hunt. It is interesting to note that the name and phone number of one FBI agent, James P. Hosty, was found in Oswald's address book and this same agent took part in the Kennedy assassination investigations. It appears Oswald was in contact with, or at least closely observed by, the intelligence community. There is even a theory, supported by photographs, suggesting that Oswald never went to the Soviet Union but was impersonated by an intelligence officer on a secret mission.

It is interesting to note that in the three years following the assassination, no less than eighteen material witnesses died—only two from natural causes and over half from violent deaths. (Six died of gunfire wounds; three died in car accidents; two committed suicide; one died of a cut throat; one died from a karate chop; and three died of heart attacks.)

The number of critics of the Warren Commission's findings has been growing. Both before the Commission hearings and after, Governor Connally himself maintained that he had been shot from the front by a different bullet than the one which struck the president; indeed, there were no less than fifty-two eyewitnesses each of whom maintained that a shot had come from in front of the motorcade. Hard evidence, corroborative eyewitness accounts and many key questions unanswered would all heavily cast doubt on the Commission's one gun, one assassin theory and would strongly suggest that there was at least one other assassin at Dealey Plaza on November 22, 1963.

In addition to all that went before, there has been much recent specific speculation, both official and unofficial, regarding the possibility of a direct Cuban link to the assassination. Cuban Premier Fidel Castro himself has commented on the events in Dallas in such a manner as to elicit serious contemplation of his country's complicity. Certainly thirteen years after the event, the United States as a country is mature enough to withstand whatever trauma might result from a new and decisive investigation—one that would finally put all speculation to rest and leave us with the truth□

Senator John Kennedy sailing at Hyannis Port with his fiancée, Jacqueline Bouvier

The Kennedy family, 1934
(L–R, front: Patricia, Joseph and Rose Kennedy
with Edward, Rosemary, Eunice, Kathleen.
Rear: John, Jean, Robert.)

Opposite above: The Kennedy family, 1937
(L–R seated: Joseph, Sr., Patricia, Jean, Eunice,
Kathleen, Edward, Joseph, Jr., Rose.
Standing: John, Robert, Rosemary.)

Opposite below: The Kennedy family, 1960
(L–R seated: Eunice Shriver, Rose and Joseph
Kennedy, Jacqueline Kennedy, Edward.
Standing: Ethel Kennedy, Stephen and Jean Smith,
President-elect John F. Kennedy, Robert,
Patricia Lawford, Sargent Shriver, Joan Kennedy,
Peter Lawford.)

President and Mrs. Kennedy and Texas Governor Connally just after arriving at Dallas's Love Field on the morning of November 22, 1963

Above: A radiant Jacqueline Kennedy, holding a bouquet of red roses, and President Kennedy are greeted by crowds at the airport

Below: Accompanied by Governor and Mrs. Connally, the president and the first lady smile from their open-topped limousine as the motorcade takes them into Dallas

Above: Mrs. Kennedy, her clothes splattered with her husband's blood, watches with Robert Kennedy as the president's body is placed in an ambulance following the flight from Dallas to Washington, D.C.

Below: November 23, the new president, Lyndon Baines Johnson, wears the anxieties of the tragic hours that have elapsed since the assassination

Inside the sixth-floor window of the Texas School Book Depository Building, from where the assassin was believed to have fired

Dealey Plaza in downtown Dallas; the Maltese cross marks the spot where President Kennedy was fatally hit

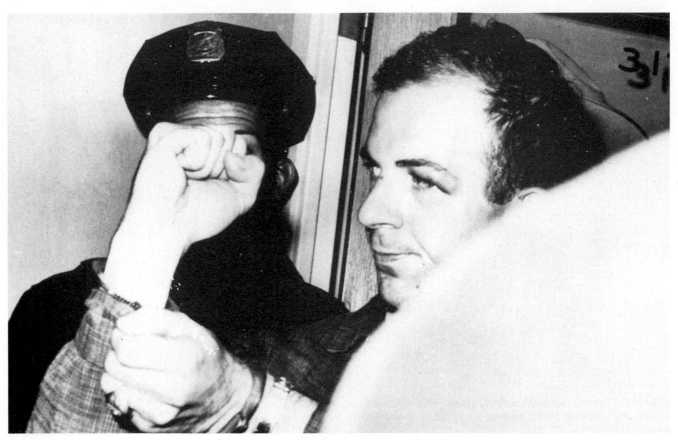

Above: Lee Harvey Oswald, the alleged single assassin, at Dallas Police Headquarters

Below and opposite above: In this film sequence which was played live to television audiences, Jack Ruby, gun in hand, lunges through a crowd of police and newsmen to shoot Oswald

Below: Oswald is placed in an ambulance after being shot

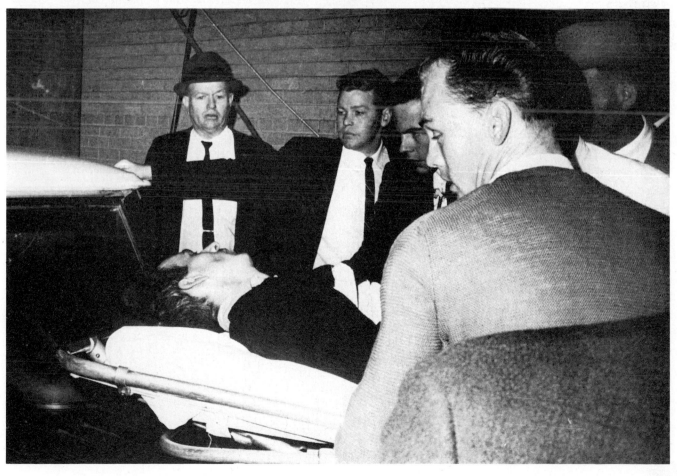

Left: Jack Ruby after fatally shooting Lee Harvey Oswald

Opposite: Mrs. Jacqueline Kennedy with her children, Caroline and John (saluting), and Robert Kennedy after funeral services for the slain president. Behind are Senator Edward Kennedy and actor Peter Lawford, the president's brother-in-law.

Below left: Warren Commission exhibit No. 134 shows Oswald holding a rifle and carrying a revolver at his hip. This photo has been the source of speculation that Oswald was impersonated by another man.

Below: Oswald's mother, Marguerite Oswald (L), and his wife, Marina, holding their infant son

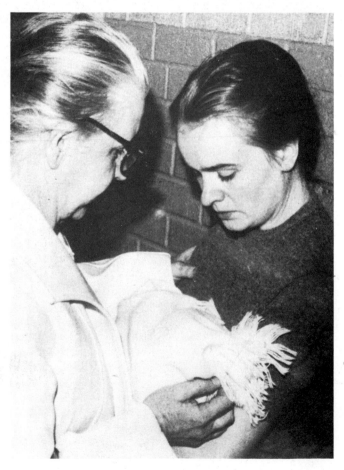

The funeral procession moving up Connecticut Avenue; Mrs. Kennedy, members of the Kennedy family and dignitaries from all over the world walk behind the caisson and the riderless horse

A wife, brother and mother mourn— eulogies at Arlington National Cemetery, November 25

Robert Kennedy places a single flower on his brother's grave, marked by an eternal flame, on the first anniversary of John Kennedy's assassination

Opposite: Two brothers share a moment

MALCOLM X

Born May 19, 1925 Omaha, Nebraska
Died February 21, 1965 New York City

Leading black civil rights leader; a minister in the Black Muslim movement; founded the Muslim Mosque, Inc. sect after breaking with Black
Muslim ideology in 1964

Alleged assassins:
Talmadge Hayer, hired assassin, 22 years old
Norman 3X Butler, member of the Black Muslims, 27 years old
Thomas 15X Johnson, member of the Black Muslims, 30 years old

Born Malcolm Little on May 19, 1925, in Omaha, Nebraska, Malcolm X was the son of a Jamaican-born Baptist preacher and a West Indian mother. From his maternal grandfather who was white, Malcolm inherited his reddish brown hair—thus gaining him the nickname Big Red. After his father's death, he was sent to a state institution in Mason, Michigan and was one of the top students in the eighth grade. He traveled to Boston and then to New York where he lived the life of a hustler who drank, took drugs, pimped and ran numbers. To support his cocaine habit he carried out a string of Boston burglaries that resulted in a prison term. During his stay at the state prison in Charlestown, Massachusetts, Malcolm became interested in the Black Muslim movement and began to correspond with its head, Elijah Muhammad. When he got out of jail Malcolm moved to Chicago where the religious cult's headquarters was located. Proving himself to be an effective speaker, he advanced up the Black Muslim hierarchy and headed Mosque No. 7 in New York City. He preached black supremacy and strict segregation of the black and white races, beliefs professed by the Black Muslims.

However internal power plays within the group resulted in Malcolm X's being suspended as a minister by Elijah Muhammad on November 23, 1963. The suspension was supposedly precipitated by Malcolm X's remark that President Kennedy's death was a case of "the chickens coming home to roost". On March 8 of the following year, Malcolm split completely with the Black Muslims and formed his own congregation as the Muslim Mosque, Inc. He continued to preach but his views were undergoing changes, and because he did not want to cut off new and important sources of support, he began to feel the urgency of working for a peaceful coexistence between the races. He founded the Organization of Afro-American Unity in the spring of 1964, subscribing to the purposes of the Organization of African Unity, the Pan-African organization that supports African independence movements. Since his split with the Black Muslims, Malcolm had been the victim of harrassment, a not uncommon practice of the Black Muslims towards defectors of their faith. As recently as February 14, 1965, Malcolm's house had been set on fire. Though he denied the need or use of bodyguards, reports had it that he did indeed keep them near.

Malcolm X was to give a speech at the Audubon Ballroom in New York on February 21, 1965, seven days after the house burning. It was known that the speech was to embody Malcolm X's new hopes for a healing of racial conflict, a message in direct variance with Black Muslim beliefs. However the night before the speech, Malcolm X told his friend Alex Haley that the Black Muslims were not to blame for the house burning, and instead a greater, more threatening force was behind it all.

The events of the assassination of Malcolm X are surrounded by conflicting accounts by spectators, police and news media, and to this day, it is not conclusively known who was responsible for the assassination.

At 3:00 P.M. on February 21, 1965, Malcolm X walked onto the stage of the Audubon Ballroom and greeted the packed room with the words, "*As-salaam alaikum*" (Peace be unto you). The crowd responded, "*Wa-alaikum salaam*" (And unto you be peace). A seemingly staged disturbance immediately broke out with a handmade smoke bomb being set off and much scuffling taking place in the front rows of the audience. Malcom X and several men on stage, presumably bodyguards, were attempting to bring order when a man with a sawed-off shotgun advanced and fired rounds of buckshot through the podium, striking Malcolm X in the chest. Two other men then fired at the fallen leader.

Varying reports described how and where the three gunmen fled. Bodyguard Reuben Francis fired at one gunman who apparently fled after being wounded. He was later identified as Talmadge Hayer. The New York Herald Tribune reported that another suspect was arrested and taken to a nearby precinct for questioning, even though the police made no further information available to the press and eventually denied ever arresting a second man. Several other spectators who suffered gunshot wounds were never asked to testify. Benjamin X, who introduced Malcolm X at the beginning of the speech, disappeared and was never brought to court as a witness. The so-called bodyguards behaved strangely in not making more active pursuit of the gunmen; three of the bodyguards in fact disappeared altogether.

On January 21, 1966, the trial of Talmadge Hayer, 22 years old, also known as Thomas Hagan, and two other defendants began. Hayer testified that the other defendants at the trial were not responsible and that he and three other accomplices, unnamed, were hired to assassinate Malcolm X. Hayer, as well as relatives of his, denied that he was ever a Black Muslim, and Hayer said that the man behind the assassination was not a Black Muslim. (If true, this supports what Malcolm X himself had suggested to Alex Haley the night before he was assassinated.)

The other two defendants, Norman 3X Butler, 27 years old, and Thomas 15X Johnson, 30 years old, were both known Black Muslims. Witnesses' testimonies vary as to whether either of these two were even present at the Audubon Ballroom on February 21. Butler may have been the second suspect whose arrest police later denied altogether. The prosecution named Johnson as the first gunman who fired the shotgun. If the disturbances were staged as part of the assassination plot, more than just the three accused would have had to take part in the conspiracy.

Talmadge Hayer, Norman 3X Butler and Thomas 15X Johnson were found guilty of first degree murder. They face mandatory life sentences with a minimum required term of twenty-six years and eight months before becoming eligible for parole.

The prosecution sought to prove that the three had formed a carefully drilled assassination squad that had been ordered to kill Malcolm X as "an object lesson" to his followers. It was also strongly suggested that the order for the assassination had been given by the Black Muslim leadership, but lacking proof, no such charges were ever formally made.

That Malcolm X was preaching coexistence with whites at the end of his life is a well-known fact. What remains a mystery is who might have benefited by his death, thereby pointing the way to those who planned his assassination. A man who rose from a strictly antisocial dropout status, Malcolm X was a dynamic leader whose public career was certainly only beginning. Many feel that he was potentially the most positive force in bringing together the black and white people of America. Who can gauge the loss of such a force? □

Malcolm X exhorting a meeting of black leaders to expand the civil rights program to a human rights program, March 1964

Above: Elijah Muhammad, spiritual leader of the Black Muslims

Below: Malcolm X speaking at a Harlem rally in June 1963 in support of the civil rights movement in Birmingham, Alabama. (Poster photo shows bodies of three Black Muslims killed in Los Angeles.)

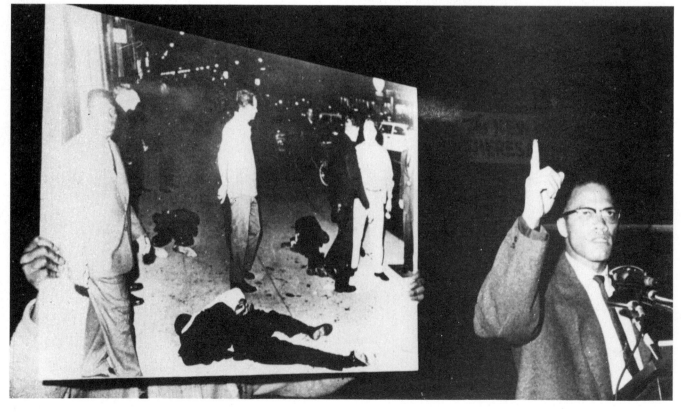

Above: Malcolm X with his daughter, Ilysah, after his return from Africa and the Middle East

Malcolm X at a press conference at Kennedy International Airport November 24, 1964

Below: An anti-segregation boycott of New York City public schools brings U.S. Congressman Adam Clayton Powell (center) together with Malcolm X

Malcolm X leaves his Queens, New York home after it had been firebombed February 14, 1965

Above: The body of Malcolm X is wheeled by police from the Audubon Ballroom where he was assassinated during a rally, February 21, 1965

Below: Talmadge Hayer, one of the alleged assassins, shot while trying to escape after the fatal shooting of Malcolm X

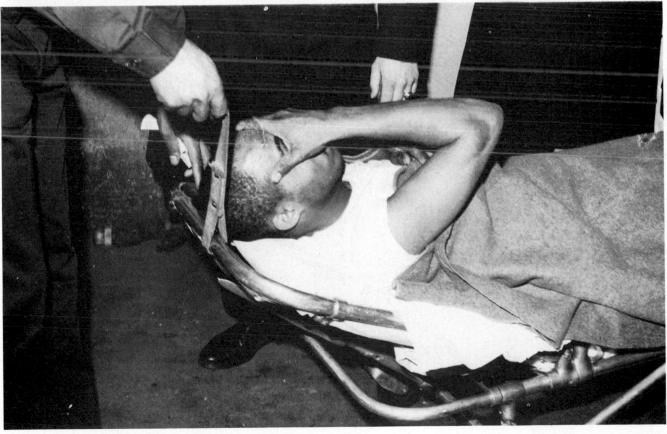

Thomas 15X Johnson, an alleged assassin

Norman 3X Butler, an alleged assassin

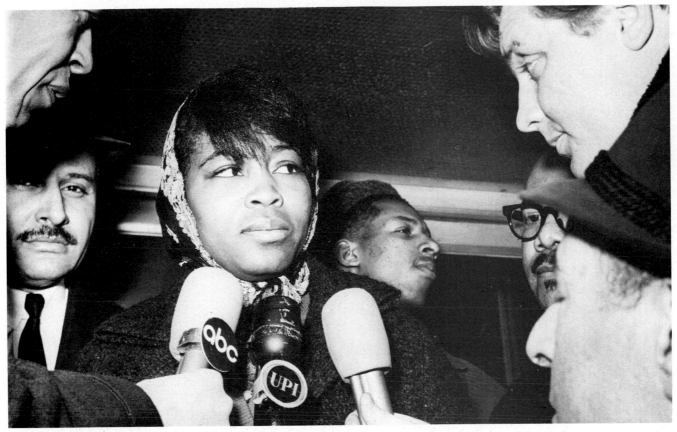

Above: Malcolm X's widow, accompanied by New York political leader Percy Sutton, arrives to view her husband's body at a funeral home, February 23

Below: The body of Malcolm X in an open casket

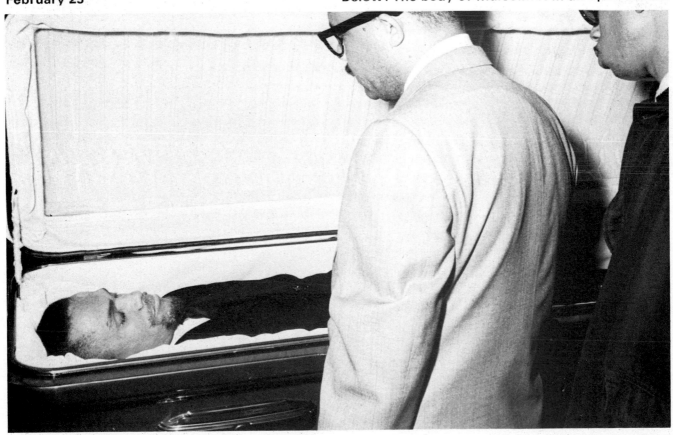

DR. HENDRIK
FRENSCH VERWOERD

Born September 8, 1901 Amsterdam, Netherlands
Died September 6, 1966 Cape Town, South Africa

Became active in South African politics as one of the leading exponents of apartheid; promulgated a series of repressive racial laws as minister of native affairs; prime minister from 1958 until his assassination in 1966

Assassin:
Demitrio Tsafendas, 48-year-old parliamentary messenger

On September 6, 1966, Dr. Hendrik Verwoerd, prime minister of South Africa, entered the paneled chamber of the House of Assembly, strode to his green leather seat and waited as the M.P.'s returned from their lunch. A parliamentary messenger in the traditional green and black uniform made his way through the crowd to the prime minister's bench. Two stilettos were tucked in his belt and a six-inch dagger was concealed in his right hand. The messenger approached Verwoerd and raised his arm as if he were about to pat him on the back. Instead, the man drew the dagger out of its leather sheath and stabbed Verwoerd three times in the chest and once in the throat. The prime minister, with blood spurting through his shirt, slumped silently over his desk. Several M.P.'s wrestled the attacker to the ground while three doctors in the room attempted to revive Verwoerd. But it was too late to save the wounded prime minister whose blood had formed puddles on the green carpet. Security officers dragged the assassin out of the chamber as he screamed, "Where's that bastard? I'll get that bastard!" The "Apostle of Apartheid" was already dead.

Verwoerd, though a leading exponent of the Afrikaner cause, was not himself a true Afrikaner since he had been born in a Dutch village near Amsterdam in 1901. His father, a grocer who had been involved in a committee to help Boer refugees in the Netherlands, decided to move his family to Cape Town and become a missionary in the Dutch Reformed Church.

When the Verwoerd family arrived in 1903, South Africa had already seen over two and a half centuries of racial conflict. In 1652 three small ships had arrived with two hundred men and a few women and children. Their assignment had been to set up a supply station for the ships of the Dutch East India Company that stopped for fresh water, meat, vegetables and repairs on the long voyages between Amsterdam and the spice-rich ports of the Far East. As time went on newcomers settled the land around Cape Town, and some intermingled with the native Hottentots and Bushmen—thus producing people whose genetic make-up the twentieth century rulers of South Africa would label "Colored". The Boers (farmers) often used the Hottentots as cheap labor, and as time went on they imported slaves from West Africa, Madagascar, Malaya, India and Ceylon. Boers interpreted the Bible as supporting the inequality of different races. Free from the control of central authority, they developed a strong sense of individualism. During the Napoleonic Wars, the Dutch ceded the Cape Colony to the British who began to occupy the area in 1806. Friction soon developed between the English-speaking settlers and the Afrikaners (those descendants of the early Dutch, French Huguenot and German settlers who spoke Afrikaans, a derivative of Dutch).

To escape the British property laws, British courts and British antislavery policies, many of the Afrikaners trekked northward out of Cape Colony into unsettled regions and into the high veld where they established their farms. In the process they ran into powerful Bantu groups that were sweeping southward. After fierce warfare, the Afrikaners defeated the Bantu but eventually ran into more difficulties as British prospectors flocked northward into the Boer republics in search of the gold and diamonds which were to make South Africa famous. It was the conservative Boer leaders' resentment against the influx of outsiders that eventually led to the Boer War from

1899 to 1902 which the British won. The Verwoerds arrived in Cape Town one year after the war's end.

In 1912 Hendrik's father was assigned to a village in Southern Rhodesia where the boy was enrolled in a British school, a circumstance that only intensified his hatred for the English. Hendrik Verwoerd was a brilliant student and received a scholarship to Britain but turned it down so that he could attend Stellenbosch University, "the center of Afrikanerdom". After doing graduate work in Hamburg, Leipzig and Berlin, Verwoerd became the first person in South Africa to receive a doctorate in mass psychology. But he obtained more than simply a degree at the University; he absorbed the Afrikaner ideology to such an extent that he was more Afrikaner than the native-born descendants of the early Dutch settlers. He began to develop the racist theories that later were put into practice as apartheid, the doctrine of separate development.

For a while Verwoerd taught psychology and then sociology at Stellenbosch, but he soon became involved in the ultranationalistic Afrikaner secret racist society, the *Broederbond*. In 1937 he joined with a young lawyer named Strijdom in founding *Die Transvaler*, an Afrikaans-language paper that was pro-Nazi during World War II. The newspaper promoted Strijdom as the only man who could save South Africa from the *swart gevaar*, the black peril. In 1948 the pro-British government was defeated, and the Nationalist party with Strijdom at its head took power. By 1950 Verwoerd was minister of native affairs and began pushing through a series of repressive racial laws. The first step had been the Population Registration Act by which every South African had to be officially classified by race so that the discrimination laws could be put into effect. These laws included the Prohibition of Mixed Marriages Act, the Immortality Amendment Act, the Separate Representation of Voters Act, the Bantus Authority Act, the Group Areas Act, the 12-Day Detention Clause, the 90-Day Detention Clause and the 180-Day Detention Clause.

According to Verwoerd's apartheid theories each racial group would have an area of the country set aside for its own separate development. The 12.4 million black Africans were to be put on special reservations from which they could venture forth only if they had special passes and proof of employment in white areas. These Bantustans made up less than 14 percent of the land and were generally areas of poor soil and meager resources. The 3.4 million

whites were to have 86 percent of the land which, of course, included those regions rich in such resources as diamonds and gold. Eventually Asians and Coloreds were also to have their own areas. The whole system of apartheid depended on massive repression, and fear of the black majority was used to get the white English-speaking and Afrikaan-speaking groups to cooperate with each other. When Strijdom died in 1958, Verwoerd took over as prime minister.

Under Verwoerd most political activity was banned, people could be imprisoned up to half a year with no charges brought against them, and the press was tightly controlled. These laws were supported by powerful police and paramilitary forces; strict enforcement of the pass laws that controlled the movement of blacks resulted in South Africa having one of the highest relative prison populations in the world. In 1960, two weeks after the savage repression of a series of protest demonstrations against the pass laws, an attempt was made upon Verwoerd's life. The would-be assassin fired two shots into the prime minister's head but he recovered within two months. World pressure on South Africa to relent in her racial policies only resulted in the country's withdrawal from the British Commonwealth. After a two-year economic slump, directly related to the break with the United Kingdom, the South African boom resumed at an even greater pace which meant more problems for Verwoerd's program. The demand for skilled workers and the lack of enough white workers meant that more and more black Africans were entering skilled professions and working in urban areas. The policy of strict segregation and exclusion of blacks from skilled jobs became ever more difficult to enforce.

What then was the motive of the assassin, an apparently white man who had been able to obtain the position of parliamentary messenger about a month before he killed Verwoerd? As it turned out, the murderer had a long history of mental illness. Demitrio Tsafendas was born in 1918 in the Portuguese colony of Mozambique, the son of an engineer from Crete and a mother whom South Africans would have regarded as mixed white and nonwhite. After receiving the equivalent of a seventh-grade education, he traveled throughout the world holding jobs only for short periods, and in 1941 he came to Cape Town and joined the merchant marine. In 1942 he went to Canada and from there illegally entered the United States by walking across a frozen river border. From 1942 until 1946 he was in a variety of American mental institutions after which he was deported to Greece, although he probably had Portuguese citizenship. He managed to travel to France, Spain, Portugal, Denmark, Sweden, England, Belgium, Turkey, Lebanon and Egypt. From 1936 onward he had suffered from the bizarre delusion that he carried an enormous tapeworm inside his body and that the worm's demands were responsible for all his irrational behavior. Tsafendas was quoted as saying, "If I did not have the tapeworm, I would not have killed Dr. Verwoerd."

In 1965 Tsafendas migrated back to South Africa where he lived with associates who were members of a religious cult called "The Followers of Jesus". They recounted how he would prepare large meals of steak, eggs, onions and tomatoes and gobble the food down like a dog without utensils; how he liked to keep his boots on in bed, and how he sprinkled chickens with water on hot days. Tsafendas described the worm as having serrated edges; he claimed that it climbed up his throat at the smell of "delicious foods" and "purred like a cat" when fed. At the trial Tsafendas was declared insane, and under the Mental Disorders Act of 1916, he was ordered detained in prison for an indefinite period.

Several questions have remained unanswered. How was Tsafendas able to obtain the five passports found among his possessions? Where did he obtain the money for his extensive travels that carried him through at least thirty countries? How was Tsafendas able to get past the screening process for the job of messenger in the Parliament building? Not only his record of schizophrenia but also the probability that he ought to have been registered as Colored, according to the racial laws, should have prevented him from obtaining the job that gave him access to Verwoerd. As far as Tsafendas's attitude toward Verwoerd's racist program is concerned, apparently he was against it until he discovered that he could pass as a white. He complained about his $140-a-month job and is supposed to have said that he was angry with Verwoerd for helping non-whites rather than poor whites such as himself.

After Verwoerd's death the apartheid policy was continued by the new prime minister Johannes Vorster who had been Verwoerd's tough minister of justice☐

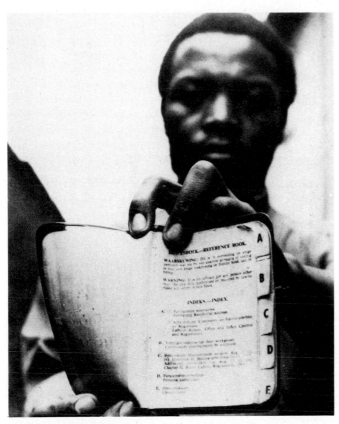

Apartheid: The most important possession for any African over sixteen years of age is his pass book; without it on his person, he can be arrested at any time

Above: Apartheid: Three languages, English, Afrikaans and Tswana, leave no doubt

Below: Apartheid: This man is taking a chance; if caught, he will face a fine of twenty dollars or twenty days in jail

Above: April 9, 1960, South African Prime Minister Hendrik Verwoerd was speaking in defense of his country's white supremacy laws. This photo was taken moments before he was shot in an attempted assassination

Below: Prime Minister Verwoerd and Basutoland (now Lesotho) Prime Minister Chief Leabua Jonathan greet each other in Pretoria, South Africa, September 2, 1966. Seeking to win for South Africa friends in independent black Africa, this marked the first time Verwoerd had played host to a black ruler

Demitrio Tsafendas, the assassin

Wrapped in a blanket, the dying prime minister is carried from Parliament after being mortally wounded, September 6, 1966

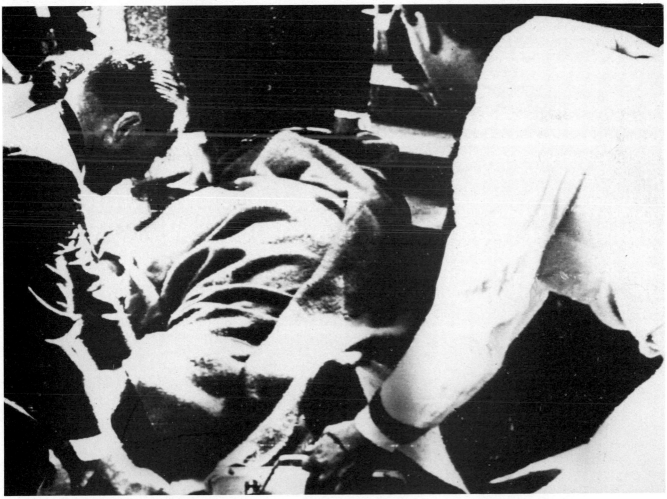

ERNESTO CHE GUEVARA

Born June 14, 1928 Rosario, Argentina
Died October 9, 1967 Bolivia

Latin American revolutionary leader; close advisor to Fidel Castro and his
Cuban rebel forces seeking the overthrow of Cuban dictator Batista;
Cuban minister of industries; leader of an abortive Bolivian guerrilla war

Assassins:
Reportedly a warrant officer sent by Bolivian President Barrientos, aided
by members of the Bolivian Rangers, an American trained counterinsurgency force

The guerrilla warfare project of Ernesto Che Guevara ended in unmitigated disaster on October 9, 1967, when he was assassinated by CIA-trained Bolivian military forces on orders from the Bolivian president. With his death the myth of "Che", which had already been carefully nurtured during his lifetime, ballooned out of all proportion to his accomplishments; he became an instant revolutionary folk hero. Actually, except for his assistance to Castro during the Cuban revolution, he had led a life of colossal failures. He mismanaged the Cuban economy; failed in his attempt to use Cuba as a base for revolutionary uprisings in Latin America; failed in his attempt to create a coordinated, broad-based revolutionary black African movement, and failed in his final project—the Bolivian guerrilla war.

Che was born in Argentina in 1925. When he was 30 years old he met Fidel and Raoul Castro in Mexico City, thus beginning a close friendship and association which would cement their lives together until Che's death. Guevara joined Castro in his guerrilla campaign against the Cuban dictator Fulgencio Batista and became the official physician of the rebel forces. Far greater than his medical services were his philosophical and tactical contributions to the revolutionary movement of the guerrillas. As a trusted comrade and in an advisory role, he had great influence with Castro. Backed by overwhelming popular support, the rebel forces were successful in overthrowing Batista's regime in 1959, and the victorious guerrillas took over the government from Havana. In 1961 Che became Cuban minister of industries and as leader of the Cuban Economics Mission, negotiated with the Soviet Union to exchange Cuban sugar for Russian oil. In December 1964 Castro and Guevara came to the U.S. as part of the Cuban delegation to the UN. The delegation rejected their quarters in a posh New York City hotel in favor of being in the city's Latin quarter.

In the mid-1960s Guevara disappeared from view, and immediately speculation arose as to where he was and what he was up to. Documents and diaries found in his possessions after his assassination record the story of the Bolivian guerrilla warfare project that was to be his downfall. Formulated in close cooperation with Fidel Castro and at all times under Castro's direct supervision, the project called for the setting up of a zone of guerrilla operations in an area of South America in which guerrillas from many countries could be trained to eventually take over their own lands.

Bolivia was selected as the base for this multi-million dollar project. It was thought that the isolated, landlocked country with its poor peasants and exploitation by foreign interests would serve as a perfect setting. It was supposed that the guerrillas would gain easy support from the impoverished peasants, the exploited workers in the mines and an urban apparatus being formed in the cities. On all three estimates Castro and Guevara were wrong. Few peasants joined the movement and, in fact, it was a peasant who betrayed their location to Bolivian military forces. While the guerrillas were able to disrupt work in the Santa Cruz oil fields, they were unable to gain support from those workers. In addition, the middle-class doctors, lawyers, dentists and university professors, who were supposed to be supporting the revolutionary movement, were ineffective. According to Castro, in his introduction to Guevara's diary, published after Guevara's death, the grand plan was being sabotaged by the leadership of the Bolivian Communist party. The party leadership in La Paz evidently dissuaded the Communist militants trained in Cuba from attempting to make contact with the guerrilla forces in the countryside. This was because the Bolivian Communist party followed the directives of the Russian Communists who rightly saw that rural terrorist guerrilla activities unsupported by a peasant base did not conform to the conditions of a Marxist urban proletariat.

But as Guevara entered Bolivia in the disguise of a bald, pipe-smoking Uruguayan businessman, he had no inkling of these shortcomings in the project. The zone selected for the guerrilla operations was along the eastern slopes of the Bolivian highlands near the border with Peru. It was thought that the area would be the perfect place to train recruits from Peru and Argentina.

In anticipation of Guevara's arrival, an advance party had acquired an abandoned cattle ranch in the base area and had begun to stock it with food and medical supplies. By January of 1967 about seventeen Cubans had arrived in Bolivia via Czechoslovakia, East Germany and Spain; their false documents allowed them entry into the country by way of Brazil, Argentina and Chile. One of the guerrilla fighters was Laura Gutierrez Bauer, an Argentinian who was a secretary in the information section of the Bolivian president's office. She was known as Tania, and after her death a cult, much like that based on Che, grew up around the story of her life in the revolutionary struggle. The training of approximately fifty men had begun. Tania was sent to Argentina on a mission to contact those who would join the guerrillas; she returned with an Argentinian who was to serve as a liaison with the movement in that country.

Castro closely supervised the activities of the guerrilla force by maintaining radio contact with Guevara. In February he sent Regis Debray, the French Marxist writer, to Bolivia in order to deliver messages that he did not want to transmit by radio. After carrying out that mission, Debray was supposed to travel to France to organize international support for the guerrilla warfare project. Instead, he was captured in April by the Bolivians, and after questioning by Bolivian and American security officers, he revealed to the world that Guevara was leading the dissident forces in Bolivia.

By early spring the guerrilla force was running into trouble. They began to realize that they would not get the support that they had expected from the peasants. In March an army patrol had discovered their base camp on the ranch and had killed two of the guerrillas in the ensuing battle. Guevara's forces managed to kill sixty soldiers in a number of ambushes, but they suffered from food and medical supply losses when they had to abandon their base camp.

One of the reasons that Castro and Guevara had selected Bolivia as the starting point for their project was that Bolivia had a poorly equipped army of about five thousand and most of that number were one year recruits. But President Barrientos was soon receiving CIA assistance in the form of a U.S. Special Forces mission that trained the Bolivian army in counterinsurgency tactics. Within five months the sixteen-man special mission, whose leader had gained experience in Laos and South Vietnam, trained a special four-hundred-man force of Rangers who put into effect their newly gained techniques. For example, a special counterinsurgency group was trained to blend in with the Indian peasants so that from August onward, they managed to keep close tabs on the guerrillas by gaining information from the people living in the area. The Bolivian army began to adopt another very effective method of ferreting out Guevara's forces: they sealed off the guerrilla zone with approximately two thousand troops and waited for the guerrillas to approach farmers or villagers for food supplies. In addition the army burned the crops of many of the area's small farms to further cut off the insurgents' food supply.

By May of 1967 Guevara's force became permanently separated into two groups when the section led by Major Juan Acuna Nuneza (Joaquin) missed a rendevous with Guevara's group. The guerrillas were becoming increasingly discouraged. They had reason to be. On June 24, 1967, the army occupied the mining communities from which the guerrillas had hoped to receive support. Twenty-five men, women and children were killed in the mining communities as the government forces arrested union leaders who they thought might have had contact with the guerrillas. The urban support that Castro had so carefully cultivated—through his agents and through the offering of "scholarships" for young people to come to Cuba to be trained in guerrilla warfare—was weakened when arrests in La Paz broke up the ring of doctors, lawyers, students and engineers.

A farmer, who had sold Joaquin's group some fish, informed the Bolivian army of their location and then agreed to lead the guerrillas into an ambush. Thus on August 31 the Joaquin group, including Tania, was wiped out. Sickness and lack of food were making Guevara's group desperate. Guevara radioed to Havana, "We have arms for another hundred men, but not a single peasant has joined up."

On October 8, 1967, a force of the American-trained Bolivian Rangers surrounded Guevara's force that was bottled up in a narrow gorge. Five members of his group managed to escape and eventually made it across the Bolivian border into Chile and from there back to Cuba. But Guevara was captured and imprisoned in a schoolhouse. At about 10:00 A.M. on October 9 President Barrientos sent an order to the troops that Ernesto Guevara should be eliminated. According to an authoritative eyewitness account, the warrant officer entered the room in the early afternoon but quickly left when confronted by Che's unintimidated stare. Soldiers outside the schoolhouse angrily urged the warrant officer to go back inside and finish the job. He returned, aimed his M-2 at Guevara and fired into Guevara's body. According to the same eyewitness account, Che raised his hands to his mouth and bit down on his fingers to stifle a scream as he slumped against the wall. Shortly thereafter other soldiers burst into the room and, firing indiscriminately, completed the execution.

On October 11 the Bolivian government released the story that Guevara had been killed in a battle on October 9. The body was soon displayed for news photographs, and within weeks a battle began over the rights to the diaries found in Guevara's belongings. The publication of those documents revealed an eleven-month struggle ending in total disaster. The plan of a small guerrilla band to foment revolution without the support of an urban proletariat or a broadly based peasantry was shown to be unfeasible, especially against a skilled counterinsurgency force.

As a footnote to history, the Bolivian ambassador to France, Joaquin Zenteno Anaya, was shot and killed in Paris on May 11, 1976. Zenteno was the general in charge of the Bolivian forces in the campaign against Guevara's guerrilla forces. A group calling itself the "International Che Guevara Brigade" reportedly claimed responsibility for Zenteno's death—giving us pause to weigh anew the impact of Che's life and beliefs, almost a decade after his death. Indeed, with the recent Cuban military successes in Africa, one wonders what role Che Guevara might have played today□

Above: Thought to be the only photo of Fidel Castro
surrounded by his guerrilla staff and troop commanders,
he is pictured here in 1957 with: (R–L) Juan Almeida;
George Sotus; Crescentio Perez, peasant leader; his
younger brother, Raoul Castro (kneeling); Universo
Sanchez; Che Guevara, and Guillermo Garcia

Below: Ernesto Che Guevara, relaxing
in the guerrillas' camp, 1958

Above: Che Guevara, his arm in a sling, arrives in Havana January 3, 1959, after the rebels had secured the capital city

Head of Cuba's economic mission, Che Guevara meets with Soviet Premier Nikita Khrushchev in Moscow, December 1960

Below: Cuban Premier Castro and Major Che Guevara (second right) during review of a peasant military parade at the former U.S. Air Force base at San Julian

Above: Touring the Middle East, Guevara meets with President Nasser in Cairo, July 1959

Below: Premier Fidel Castro links arms with Raoul Castro (3rd L) and Che Guevara (2nd L) in a May Day parade in Havana, May 1, 1964

As Cuba's Minister of Industry, Che Guevara prepares to drive to the UN as a member of the Cuban delegation, December 1964

Oozing self-confidence, Che Guevara arrives at the CBS studios to appear on ''Face the Nation''

Disregarding his notes, Che Guevara heatedly addresses the UN General Assembly concerning U.S. military presence in the Caribbean

A candid face is refreshing, if unique, in the delegates' chambers at the UN

Above: Che Guevara enjoys a cigar during an appearance on "Face the Nation"

Below: A photo shown at a meeting of the Organization of American States (OAS) was submitted as evidence that Che Guevara was leading guerrillas in Bolivia

One of the last photographs taken of Che Guevara, shown here in Bolivia with his mule, Chico, in late September 1967

Opposite: On October 10, 1967, the Bolivian Army displayed the bullet-torn body of Che Guevara, comparing it with a photograph of the guerrilla leader as proof of identification

Thought to be the last photo of Che, taken a few weeks before his assassination; he is pictured studying a map of the Pesca River region with the aid of several local Indians

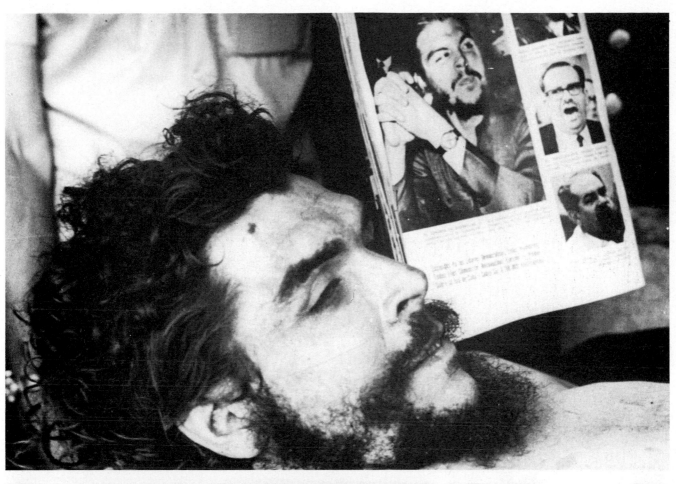

197

DR. MARTIN LUTHER KING, JR.

**Born January 15, 1929 Atlanta, Georgia
Died April 4, 1968 Memphis, Tennessee**

Black civil rights leader; active in the NAACP and head of the Southern Christian Leadership Conference; 1964 Nobel Peace Prize winner as the prime motivating force behind the nonviolent civil rights movement

**Alleged assassin:
James Earl Ray, 40-year-old escaped convict and drifter**

Dr. Martin Luther King, Jr. was one of the early forces in the South's desegregation efforts in the mid-1950s who went on to assume leadership of the civil rights movement. Few American social leaders have had such an enormous impact, realized in so short a time span. More than just a leader, King represented a moral force, effectively drawing on the philosophies of brotherly love of mankind and on nonviolence, and inspiring the black and white communities to take action together. He was awarded the Nobel Peace Prize in 1964 and was one of the first in the country to lend his great prestige and moral force to the anti-Vietnam movement, speaking out against the United 'States' involvement long before it was even considered an acceptable, much less a necessary, position for a man of conscience to assume. Almost anticlimactically, the 1968 Civil Rights Act was enacted immediately after his violent death shocked the country.

Born in 1929, King grew up in Atlanta in a middle-class black neighborhood where his father was pastor of the Ebenezer Baptist Church and well respected in his community. After attending Morehouse College, Crozer Theological Seminary and later receiving his doctorate from Boston University —during which time he was influenced by the philosophies of Hegel, Marx, Neibuhr, Sartre and especially Gandhi—he became a pastor in Montgomery, Alabama. Involved in the local NAACP (National Association for the Advancement of Colored People), he headed in 1955 the successful organization of ongoing protest efforts against segregation practices in Montgomery. In 1957 he formed the Southern Christian Leadership Conference (SCLC), and as its leader King's influence spread to the extent that the isolated efforts of blacks to obtain equal rights became strengthened and solidified into one movement.

However in the 1960s a growing number of mostly young, educated and militant blacks became increasingly impatient with nonviolence as an effective tactic for achieving equality and became openly critical of the nonviolent philosophy as a rallying point for the black community. Less willing to deal with whites and subscribing to more militant confrontation, this group put great pressure on King and his supporters to maintain both solidarity in the ranks while holding to a nonviolent approach to their goals.

It was for this reason that King came to Memphis in April of 1968—to stage a successful, nonviolent strike protest in support of black sewer and garbage collectors against the city and thereby to confront his critics on the issue of the effectiveness of non-violence.

While in Memphis for the protest march, Dr. King was staying at the black-owned Lorraine Motel on the edge of Memphis's black district. His mind was focused ahead toward the Poor People's Campaign scheduled to march on Washington D.C. on April 29. This was to be an all-out effort to force the attention of Congress toward addressing the problems of poverty and racism. He badly needed a successful protest here in Memphis to gain support among blacks and pave the way for the march to Washington.

On April 4, 1968, in the early afternoon, James Earl Ray rented a room in a cheap boardinghouse where a bathroom window gave him a clear, unobstructed view of Room 306 of the Lorraine Motel some 200 yards away—the room occupied by King. Waiting with his .243-caliber Remington rifle with its powerful 2×4 scope, purchased the week before in Alabama, Ray watched through field binoculars, maintaining his death vigil until he could fulfill his mission.

Room 306, which King was sharing with his associate in the civil rights movement, Dr. Ralph Abernathy, had been the headquarters all day for a round of staff meetings. They had been waiting to hear the ruling of a federal court on an injunction to stop the Memphis march, planned in several days. At 5:40 P.M. they were in their room preparing to go to dinner at the home of a friend, the Reverend Billy Kyle, who had arrived to pick them up. They had been reminiscing about past times together and ironically about threats on King's life. A few minutes before 6:00 King walked out onto the second-story balcony, greeting his colleagues who were in the courtyard below. Leaning on the railing and joking with his friends, he had just called out to Ben Branch, the singer in the band for the night's planned rally, to sing "Precious Lord". "Sing it real pretty," he admonished. Then came a loud, staccato noise, as if a car had backfired close by.

King fell backward, mortally wounded, hit in his right jaw. Abernathy rushed out onto the balcony to find King still conscious and staring up at him as if somehow trying to communicate. By then those in the courtyard had rushed up the stairs and had surrounded their fallen leader, horrified at the realization that the one man who could stop all the racial violence which they so abhorred had been struck down. Joseph Louw, a young photographer who had been photographing King's campaign, was on the balcony and, grabbing his camera, shot picture after picture toward any direction from which the bullet might have come, hoping to get the killer on film.

Meanwhile Ray had left the roominghouse, dropping the rifle several doors down the street, and drove off in his white Mustang. Although police were able to locate the bathroom window as well as the weapon and get a description of Ray and his car in less than ten minutes after the shooting, Ray managed to elude capture for over two months. After one of the most intense manhunts, he was arrested on June 8 at London's Heathrow International Airport, having traveled all over Canada and Europe under, it was later learned, many aliases.

The alleged sole assassin, James Earl Ray, born in 1928, came from a poor and unstable family in Illinois. After his "general" discharge from military service, where he was considered a disciplinary problem, he fell into a career of crime and spent most of the next twenty years in and out of jail. Considered a smalltimer, he never was known to fire the gun he usually carried during his crimes. He escaped from the Missouri State Penitentiary in April of 1967 and drifted around the country and into Canada and Mexico.

There is evidence that he accumulated a large sum of money while at the penitentiary, and it has been suggested that he could have obt .ined it from drug trafficking or possibly as a knowing or unsuspecting tool of some conspiracy. There is so far insufficient evidence to link him with such a conspiracy or even to identify the nature and motives of such a conspiracy if one existed. However, the three possibilities suggested are the Ku Klux Klan or one of its member organizations; some local Memphis group fearful of the strike; some militant black group—each of which, one could conjecture, had motives for wanting King eliminated.

It is unlikely that the national Ku Klux Klan organization would have attempted to have the civil rights leader killed, especially as the Klan's leadership was aware of the degree to which the FBI has infiltrated it's organization. However, since the Klan is in reality a loosely organized group of affiliated memberships, it is possible that some maverick group may have taken it upon itself to have King assassinated without the prior knowledge or blessing of the national organization.

It is unlikely that any reasonably responsible Memphis group would have planned an assassination, as the disruption caused by the death of the civil rights leader would have been far greater than the impending strike. It is difficult to imagine Ray's link with a Memphis group insofar as he supposedly received money a year in advance of the 1968 assassination when no one could have anticipated a garbage collector's strike.

As to the third suggested conspiracy theory, there is evidence that several radical black groups made attempts on the lives of more moderate black leaders. However, the likelihood of such a group employing or even contacting someone like Ray to do the job is implausible.

In the light of the assassinations of both John F. Kennedy and Robert F. Kennedy, there is another school of thought that suggests a conspiracy of some extreme right-wing element of national political thought in the United States—organizing itself with the express purpose of eliminating from the national leadership any liberal who had achieved a genuine, widespread base of support with the poor and essentially disenfranchised, whose potential coalescence under such a leader could present a very real threat to the maintenance of the right wing as a political force. In other words, stop the revolution by killing the leader.

Newly revealed information adds to the mystery surrounding King's death. The U.S. Senate Intelligence Committee revealed that the FBI began serious surveillance of King in 1959. Starting in October of 1963 it began to tap King's telephone and in January of 1964 it placed listening devices in his offices and hotel rooms. J. Edgar Hoover reportedly told associates that he suspected Dr. King of associating with a known Communist who, it was feared, might influence him and the civil rights movement. It was also thought that Hoover disliked King's criticism of him for not protecting black civil rights workers in the South. Hoover publicly labeled King a "liar" and privately called him a "degenerate". Hoover stated that King's Southern Christian Leadership Conference was a "black hate group". In 1964 counterintelligence chief William C. Sullivan wrote to Hoover that it was time to knock King "off his pedestal", and from 1964 until his death the FBI maintained eight known wiretaps and sixteen bugs on King. The FBI tried to convince a college not to grant him an honorary degree; they tried to prevent his having an audience with Pope Paul VI, and they devoted some effort to developing a black leader to replace King once he had been discredited.

The now famous form of harassment that proved most shocking to the public was a letter sent to King thirty-four days before he was to receive the Nobel Prize. It attempted to drive him to suicide after alluding to a recording in which King was supposedly sexually compromised. "King, there is only one thing left for you to do. You know what it is. You have just thirty-four days in which to do it. This exact number has been selected for a specific reason. It has definite practical significance. You are done. There is but one way out for you."

The FBI also planned to leak to the press that King was staying at a white-owned hotel when he was in Memphis to lead the boycott in 1968. While there is no evidence that the FBI followed through, that bit of information did appear in local papers. The result was that King moved to the black-owned Lorraine Motel where he was assassinated on April 4, 1968.

Other inconsistencies remain unexplained.

Ray told the judge, who sentenced him to ninety-nine years in prison, that by pleading guilty he was not agreeing that he had not been part of a conspiracy. Ray made statements that he had been framed by criminals and sold out by his lawyers.

How was Ray able to find the rooming house that was the perfect place from which to shoot King and to make an unimpeded getaway, since he was not familiar with Memphis? And how was he able to locate this boardinghouse in such a short time—two and a half hours from the time he arrived in Memphis until the murder.

Why was Ray so careless in leaving his fingerprints around to be easily found and identified?

What were Ray's connections in New Orleans where he claimed he made contact with criminal associates by telephone?

Ray's travel bag was discarded with his rifle on a street near where King was shot. Whose underwear was in Ray's luggage? It did not fit Ray.

Where did he get the money for his escape trip? Who was the mysterious Raoul for whom Ray said he did some smuggling in jewelry and heroin.

How did Ray travel about the world so easily with secure aliases and sufficient money?

Finally, what motive did Ray have to kill Martin Luther King alone?

We are all surely aware of the significance of Martin Luther King's life, each to his own view. But it is signally important to the future of us all that we are left with no doubt whatsoever as to the real meaning of his death. If not, we may thereby abrogate some small measure of our initiative as free people. If King was assassinated in order to somehow manipulate us as citizens, it behooves us to find out forthwith. For some of us were denied a leader we could follow, and others of us were denied a leader whose moral thrust was unacceptable, but in either case, his death constituted a loss by force that was certainly not of any thinking person's choice□

Above: Martin Luther King and his wife, together with other prominent civil rights leaders, leading the march from Selma to Montgomery, Alabama, March 1965

Below: The 1963 March on Washington; an aerial view of the demonstrators massed around Lincoln Monument and the Reflecting Pool in Washington, D.C.

King holds his head after being hit by a thrown rock at the start of a march supporting open housing on Chicago's Southwest Side, August 1966

In the Rose Garden of the White House June 22, 1963, after a meeting of civil rights leaders with President Kennedy are (L–R) King; Attorney General Robert Kennedy; Roy Wilkins, NAACP executive secretary, and Vice President Lyndon Johnson

Martin Luther King, his young son beside him, pulls up a four-foot cross, symbol of the Ku Klux Klan, that was burned on the front lawn of his home in Atlanta

King embraces his wife, Coretta, following the announcement that he had been awarded the Nobel Peace Prize for 1964

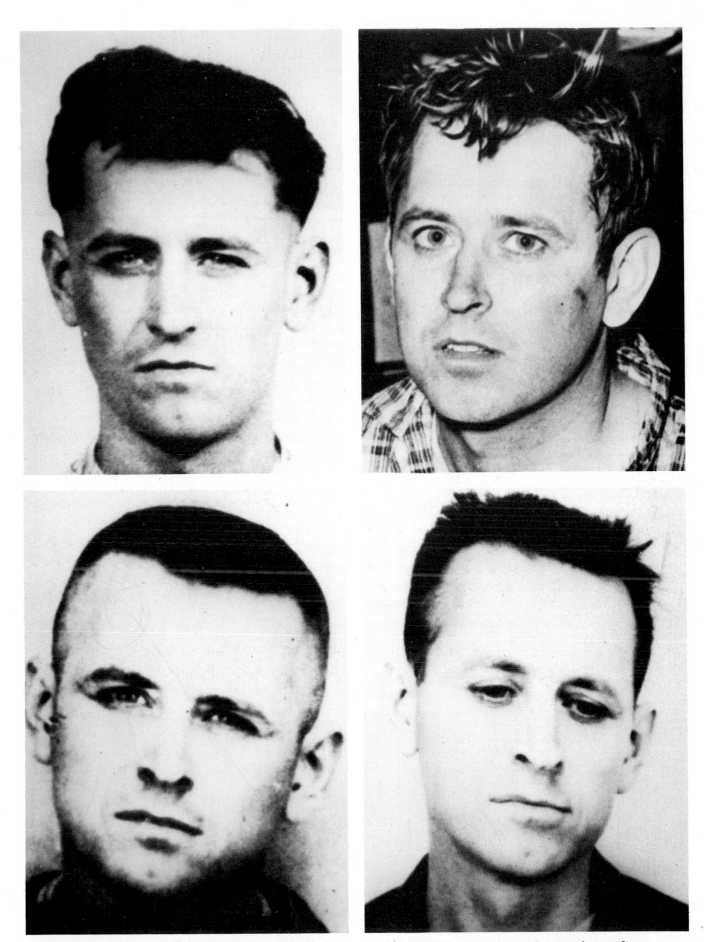

Four faces of the alleged assassin, James Earl Ray, taken while he was in various prisons from 1952 to 1966

Above: An assassin's view, through a simulated telescopic gunsight, of the balcony where King stood when assassinated; the room occupied by the civil rights leader is marked with a wreath on the door

Below: This is the view from Room 306 of the Lorraine Motel, occupied by Dr. King, looking toward the building from which the sniper's shot was said to have been fired

Opposite: Dr. Martin Luther King, Jr., in a reflective moment

ROBERT
FRANCIS KENNEDY

Born November 20, 1925 Brookline, Massachusetts
Died June 5, 1968 Los Angeles, California

U.S. senator from New York; campaigned for Democratic nomination for 1968 presidential election; former attorney general under his brother, President John F. Kennedy

Alleged assassin:
Sirhan Bishara Sirhan, 26 years old, born in Palestine

With tragic prophecy, John F. Kennedy once said, "I ran for Congress to take the place of my brother Joe. If anything happens to me, Bobby will take my place. And if Bobby gives out, there is Teddy coming along." So it was that Robert Francis Kennedy, 42 years old, seventh of Rose and Joseph Kennedy's nine children, and with his two older brothers dead before him, set out to become president of the United States.

Robert Kennedy's whole life had been geared for the challenge of politics. After serving in the Navy, he graduated from the University of Virginia Law School and, by the age of 27, had already served as a prosecutor for the Criminal Division of the U.S. Justice Department and managed his brother John's campaign for a seat in the U.S. Senate. He then worked for the Senate Permanent Investigations Subcommittee, chaired by Senator Joseph McCarthy, and in a reversal of roles which would from then on categorize him in some eyes as ruthless, he became chief counsel for a sub-committee investigating the same Senator McCarthy and his practices of communist "witch hunting". He also gained national status as the man who convicted teamsters' union boss Jimmy Hoffa. Following John Kennedy's successful campaign for president in 1960, he became attorney general of the United States, offering, as many felt, a sober and substantial balance to some of the more casual activities of Camelot.

After his brother's death he became U.S. senator from New York, waging a grueling and deft campaign against a popular and well-respected Republican incumbent, Senator Kenneth Keating. It was during this time that his own political focus began to come clear. From the pragmatic campaign organizer and political wheeler-dealer that had categorized his behind-the-scenes behavior with his brother John, he gradually found his own unique roots with the people, transforming him into an idealistic humanitarian whose political drive evolved from responding to the desperate needs of the oppressed.

When Lyndon Johnson removed himself from the 1968 presidential race, Kennedy declared his candidacy. His rapid move to the head of the field was spurred by his seemingly magical ability to communicate to an electorate that apparently was ready for his brand of idealism, his visions of conferring dignity to the dispossessed of America. He often expressed his political creed by quoting, "Some men see things as they are and say why. I dream things that never were and say, why not."

He had just won the vital California primary; shortly after midnight on June 5, Kennedy was addressing a crowd at a victory celebration in the Embassy Ballroom of the Ambassador Hotel in downtown Los Angeles.

The large room was packed with exuberant campaign workers and supporters who crowded around the stage where a jubilant Kennedy, his wife, Ethel, standing near him, was saying a few words of thanks to his workers and volunteers and offering congratulations to his Democratic opponent, Senator Eugene McCarthy. He also emphasized his gratitude to Cesar Chavez, leader of the migrant farm workers, whose cause Kennedy had strongly espoused and on whose behalf Ethel Kennedy had become actively involved.

Leaving the ballroom, Kennedy and his wife with staff and aides, including athletes Roosevelt "Rosie" Grier and Rafer Johnson, and a local private bodyguard, Thane Cesar, made their way into a corridor which would lead them through a hotel kitchen to another room where a press conference was scheduled.

Waiting in the narrow, fluorescent-lit kitchen corridor were several television cameramen; the maître d'hôtel, Carl Uecker, and hotel employees, Jesus Perez and Juan Romero. Also waiting was Sirhan Bishara Sirhan, armed with his .22-caliber eight-shot Iver Johnson pistol. Each man waited for his own purpose.

Shaking hands as he went, Kennedy was moving slowly down the corridor when Sirhan fired: once, twice, crying out something unintelligible. He fired all eight shots before he was tackled from every side to screams of "Rafer, get the gun—get the fucking gun!" Kennedy lay mortally wounded and five others in the corridor sustained bullet wounds. Rafer Johnson and Rosie Grier had grabbed Sirhan as much to protect him from the shocked and furious crowd as to subdue him. Ethel Kennedy knelt by her husband, trying to keep the crushing crowd away. Kennedy's only words were, "How bad is it?" Juan Romero placed a rosary in his hands. Kennedy had been hit by three bullets, two entering his armpit and another entering the right mastoid from behind his left ear. He was rushed in an ambulance to Los Angeles Central Receiving Hospital and later to the Good Samaritan Hospital for massive brain surgery. The damage, however, was too great and Senator Robert F. Kennedy died.

Even now there are many unexplained inconsistencies and counter evidence that dispute the single assassin theory which was the official finding.

In all, ten bullets were recovered from the assassination scene: two of the three bullets fired at Kennedy lodged in his brain and neck; five bullets lodged in each of the five other people hit (Paul Schrade, Elizabeth Evan, Ira Goldstein, Irwin Stroll and William Weisel); three bullets were recovered from different locations in the kitchen area. Sirhan's pistol could only fire eight shots without reloading, which he did not have the opportunity to do. Since there were two bullets unaccounted for, it is apparent that at least one other weapon was fired at the time. Simple arithmetics argues against the official finding!

In the official medical report, Dr. Thomas Noguchi concluded that the bullet entering Kennedy's right mastoid and penetrating the brain was the cause of death. It was Dr. Noguchi's expert opinion, given in testimony at the investigation, that the fatal bullet was fired at a range of not more than two or three inches from Kennedy's head. However, no witness who testified ever placed Sirhan any closer to the senator than two feet during the time he was firing his pistol. Thane Cesar, the security guard, was standing directly behind Kennedy and admitted drawing his gun after Sirhan began firing. Cesar conceded his gun might have gone off, but asserted that he did not shoot at Kennedy. Why has his gun not been test-fired for comparison?

Criminologist William W. Harper compared the bullet which entered Kennedy's armpit and lodged in the neck with the bullet removed from William Weisel and found that the bullets had no common characteristics and sharply differing rifling marks— indicating that the bullets could not have come from the same gun. Further, Harper stated that, based on the available evidence, Kennedy was shot at least once from a position completely removed from where Sirhan was standing. Harper therefore concluded that a second weapon was involved and that two different firing postures were used in the shootings. His findings and conclusions are supported by a number of other authoritative experts, including three other qualified criminologists (Drs. Herbert L. MacDonell, Vincent P. Quinn and Lowell Bradford).

Sirhan's weapon has never been test-fired, as is usual with standard police procedure, to determine whether or not the recovered bullets were all fired from Sirhan's weapon. In fact, the head of the Los Angeles Police Department Criminology Laboratory unexplainably refused to test-fire the gun during investigations.

A young woman in a white polka-dot dress was seen with Sirhan in the hotel kitchen but left shortly before Kennedy started out of the Embassy Ballroom. A campaign worker, Sandy Serrano, saw a woman in a white polka-dot dress, accompanied by two other people, pass her and enter the hotel while Kennedy was speaking in the ballroom. Serrano, still outside after the shooting, saw these same people race out of the hotel and, according to Serrano, the woman in the polka-dot dress shouted, "We shot him! We shot Kennedy!" Cathy Fulmer, a woman the police produced as a possible suspect, was not identified by Serrano as the same woman she had seen; Cathy Fulmer was found dead in a motel room several days after the conviction of Sirhan. There is no conclusive finding about her death.

The alleged assassin, Sirhan Bishara, was born March 19, 1944, in Jordan. A common name for the area, Sirhan means variously "wolf", "wanderer" or "one who grazes"; Bishara was his father's first name. As is the Arab custom, Sirhan did not use a family name so at the age of 12, when he came with his parents to the U.S., for want of a last name, he doubled his first name to become Sirhan Bishara Sirhan. The family lived in Pasadena, California, where Sirhan attended high school and then Pasadena City College for a short time. Slight of frame, 5 feet 2 inches, 120 pounds, he hoped to become a jockey and started apprenticeship at Hollywood Park as a horse boy. Later, as tensions mounted between Jordan and Israel over the Palestinians, Sirhan was known to be deeply concerned over the matter. The occupations and whereabouts of Sirhan are unclear in the later part of 1967 and into 1968, but among his belongings were later found several newspaper clippings which defamed Robert Kennedy, along with careful records of where Kennedy would be appearing during the California primary campaign. In his dairy was the entry, "Robert Kennedy must be killed before June 5, 1968."

In searching for motivations to explain why the Jordanian–born Sirhan would have attempted to assassinate Senator Kennedy, many people focused on the Palestinian tensions and the fact that Kennedy strongly supported a pro-Israel stance. There were the clippings and the diary memos which lend support to this idea. However as of this writing, Sirhan is, according to doctors, unable to recall drawing or firing a gun on June 5. Doctors contend that inability to recall an act, either consciously or at some subconscious level, can indicate either mental disorder or some kind of programing input or behavioral modification, caused by an external influence acting with deliberation. With no history of mental disorders, the possibility of a conspiracy involved in programing the alleged single assassin simply cannot be dismissed.

John F. Kennedy, Martin Luther King, Jr., Robert F. Kennedy. Three liberal national leaders, each with a unique ability to evoke seemingly unqualified loyalty and response from the poor and needy in spirit as well as means. All assassinated, removed from positions of influence in a great democratic society with no history of such national violence as part of the political process.

The United States as a country, as an entity, is ultimately the reflection of all its people. A national attitude is accomplished only after the people reflect and react. Every citizen is responsible in part for the quality of such a national attitude. If the United States is prepared to accept assassination as a legitimate political tool, it will do so only after the people as individuals have so decided. Unfortunately, as is so often the case when freedom is casually accepted as a matter of divine right, capacity for outrage becomes dulled, and national purpose sinks when confronted with individual lack of purpose.

If the single assassin theory in each of these cases is truly viable, then Americans are sadly less than vocal about outlawing the outlaws, about insisting that the leadership think anew the practical means of erasing this aberration from the political arena. More security guards are *not* the answer—first must come the genuine outrage and then the firm purpose.

There is much that substantiates a challenge to the single assassin theory in all three cases, and voices crying in the wilderness are not the answer. It is time to once and for all declare every past investigation invalid, beginning with the most golden of all, the Warren Commission; unassailable, independent inquiries, free to wander down all the corridors of suspicion, should be instituted immediately. And no more political games. Drive the rascals out of the halls of justice. Let the watchword be: protect none but the innocent. Let it begin, and end, and let the final judgment of America as a people be enlightened by whatever truths emerge□

Above: Senate Rackets Committee Counsel Robert F. Kennedy (L) and committee member Senator John F. Kennedy, talking with youngest brother, Edward, during a 1959 committee investigation

Below: Attorney General Robert F. Kennedy with his brother, President John F. Kennedy in 1963

Bobby, 12, and Teddy, 6, at school in London in 1938 while their father,
Joseph P. Kennedy, was U.S. ambassador to the Court of St. James

Kennedy poses for the camera with his 16-month-old son Christopher and four-year-old daughter Kerry, during his 1964 senatorial election campaign

U.S. Senator-elect Robert F. Kennedy, his wife and children on an outing to the Bronx Zoo. In front (L–R) Mary, 8; the senator-elect; Kerry, 5, and Michael, 6. In the middle (L–R) David, 9, and Robert, 11. In back (L–R) Joseph, 12; Kathleen, 13, and Mrs. Kennedy

The Attorney General announces to newsmen in 1961 that he is sending two hundred more federal marshalls to Montgomery, Alabama because of the racial violence there

Robert Kennedy at the summit of 13,900-foot Mt. Kennedy, the Canadian peak named in honor of his brother, the late President Kennedy

Kennedy magic—campaigning in Sacremento, California for
the Democratic nomination for president, May 1968

Senator Kennedy and his wife, Ethel, at the Ambassador Hotel, June 5, prior to making his victory speech after winning the California primary; within minutes he was to be gunned down by an assassin's bullets

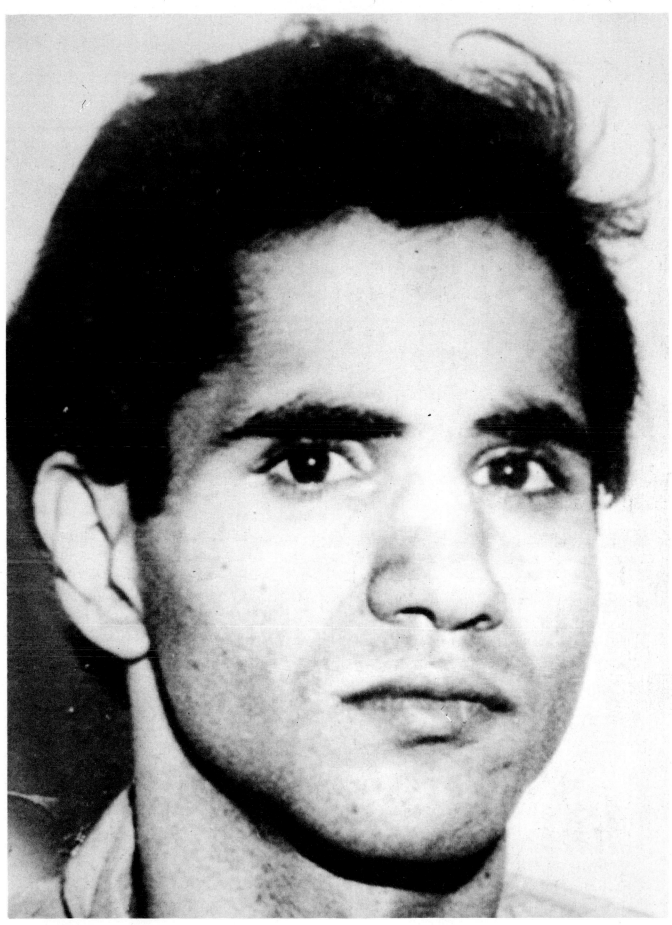

Sirhan Bishara Sirhan, the assassin

Above: The crowd, with ex-football player
Roosevelt Grier in the foreground, grabbing
Sirhan after he began shooting

Above right: Sirhan being taken from the
Ambassador Hotel following the shooting

In Amman, Jordan, the father of Sirhan studies
a Jordanian magazine which bears a picture
of his son

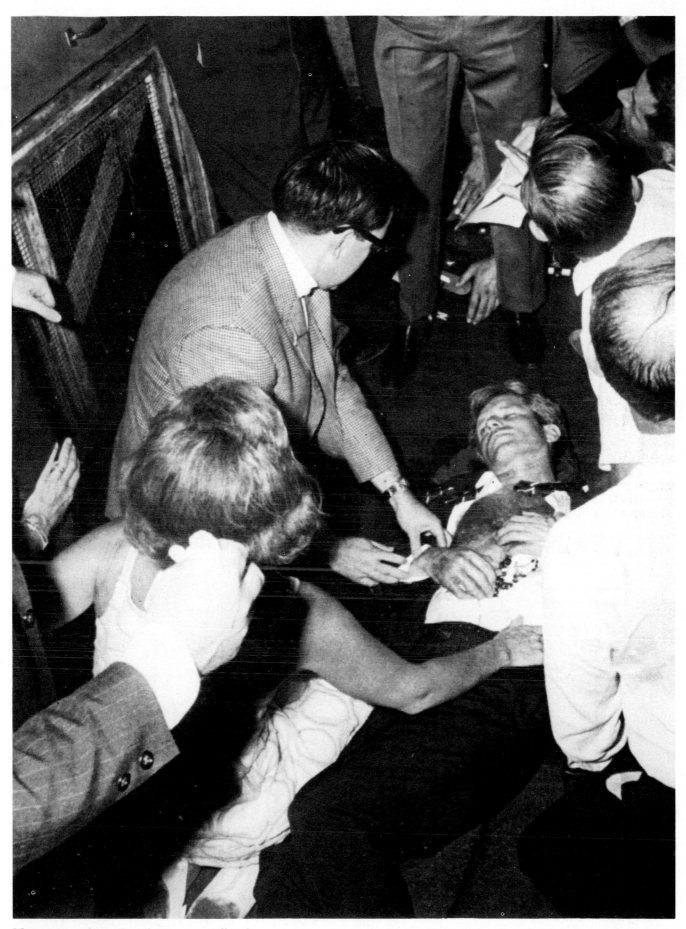

Moments after the shots were fired

Family members bringing the casket home:
(L–R) Jean Kennedy Smith; Kathleen Kennedy;
Pat Kennedy Lawford; Robert Kennedy, Jr.
(looking down); Rafer Johnson; Senator Edward
Kennedy; Jacqueline Kennedy, and Ethel Kennedy

Jacqueline Kennedy and her children, Caroline
and John, Jr., touch Robert Kennedy's coffin
in St. Patrick's Cathedral,
New York City

Edward Kennedy, Ethel Kennedy and Joseph P. Kennedy

Following private services at St. Patrick's Cathedral, Ethel Kennedy leaves with Edward Kennedy and her oldest son, Joseph, beside her and Mrs. Rose Kennedy following behind

A last farewell—the hearse bearing the body of Robert Kennedy pauses a moment between Resurrection City of the Poor People's Campaign and Lincoln Memorial en route to Arlington National Cemetery for final burial

TOM MBOYA

Born August 15, 1930 Luoland
Died July 5, 1969 Nairobi, Kenya

A founder and general secretary of the KANU, Kenya's ruling political party; leader in Kenya's efforts for independence and national unity; minister of economic planning and development; probable successor to President Jomo Kenyatta had he lived

Alleged assassin:
Nahashon Isaac Njenga Njoroye, member of the Kikuyu tribe

On July 5, 1969, 38-year-old Tom Mboya, Kenya's minister of economic planning and development, entered a busy downtown Nairobi drugstore for some casual shopping. As he left the store a few minutes later, an automobile, reportedly carrying three men, pulled over to the curb next to where he was standing. One of the men jumped out of the car and gunned him down. The young political leader was rushed to the hospital, his suede jacket soaked with blood, his hapless bodyguard weeping ineffectual tears over him. He died the same day of a bullet that had struck him in the chest. When he died he was the third most powerful man in the Kenyan government.

Kenya's population consisted of about ten million people from a variety of different tribal backgrounds. The largest tribe, and the dominant one in politics, was the Kikuyu tribe which numbered about two million. The founding president and by far the most outstanding political leader of Kenya was Jomo Kenyatta, a Kikuyu. Kikuyus filled most of the top civil service positions and several of the important governmental ministries. Kikuyus were considered more aggressive and better educated than members of other tribes.

The second largest tribal group in Kenya were the Luos with about 1.3 million people. The Luos had always felt that the Kikuyus held a disproportionate share of the power and positions and Tom Mboya was a Luo.

The tribal conflict was complicated by a political division that did not strictly follow tribal divisions. Mboya had been a founder and general secretary of the ruling party—the Kenya African National Union (KANU), a party with large Kikuyu support. On the other hand many of the Luos were split in their party loyalties. Some, such as Mboya, joined the KANU; others, perhaps a majority of the Luos, followed the lead of Oginga Odinga, a Luo chief and leader of the opposition party—the Kenya People's Union (KPU).

President Kenyatta, Vice President Daniel Arap Moi and Economics Minister Mboya all belonged to the KANU, while tribalists, such as Odinga, believed that all Luos should support the KPU. Odinga and Mboya had thus become very hostile political enemies.

At Mboya's funeral the revived tribal animosities were plainly evident. "Tom, why did you join with them?" the people shouted in Luo as the funeral procession brought the body back to Luoland. For the first time, Jomo Kenyatta, the 80-year-old Kikuyu president, was jeered in public. The *Mzee*— or Grand Old Man—had always been revered as the founder of independent Kenya, and such public disapproval was, until then, unheard of.

But tribal differences were not the only causes of political hatred. Mboya had had a spectacular political career, and while gaining great popularity among the people, he had also, not unnaturally, created many enemies. At the age of 22 in 1952, while working as a sanitation inspector in Nairobi, he helped organize African employees of the British colonial government. He was only 23 years old when elected secretary of the Kenya Federation of Labor. During the 1950s, while Jomo Kenyatta was under detention on charges of directing the Mau Mau (considered by the British a terrorist organization, by Kenyans a genuine revolutionary movement), Mboya was free and continued to gain prominence. In 1958 he was elected chairman of the All-African Peoples Conference in Accra, Ghana, a meeting designed by President Kwame Nkrumah of Ghana to create and encourage African nationalist movements.

Mboya was one of the leaders in the movement for freedom, *uhuru*, but he did not agree with the violent tactics of the Mau Mau uprisings against the British. Yet when Kenyatta was under detention and Mboya was getting all the publicity, he was firm in declaring that Kenyatta should be the first leader of the soon to be independent country. Mboya, however, can certainly be considered one of the founding fathers of his country—for instance, he was the architect of many of Kenya's important documents including Kenya's constitution.

As is often the case with politicians, however, genuine political differences are often infused with a strictly "me or him" sense of survival, and Mboya was resented mightily by many African politicians primarily because of his popularity, both within and outside Africa. His handsome features put him on the covers and front pages of the magazines and newspapers wherever he went. It has been said that Mboya's cold and arrogant manners alienated many possible allies. The young Kikuyu politicians resented the fact that Mboya was out winning popularity when the British had banned all political activity for Kikuyus. In 1962 Mboya minced no words: "There is no doubt that the young Kikuyu intellectuals are against me. I am aware of this. It is nothing new. The problem is that there is no second man to Kenyatta whom they see as the leader of the Kikuyus. I represent a threat to them."

Still another cause of dissention was the fact that Mboya was pro-Western. He had studied a year at Oxford and felt at ease with the leaders of the Western democracies. While being opposed to many of the policies of China and the Soviet Union, his political opponent Odinga thus had not only tribalist leanings which Mboya resented, but also a leftist political orientation that Mboya resisted. Mboya stood for a moderate socialism based upon a mixed economy. The rivalry and mutual animosity between Odinga and Mboya were so great that Odinga worked for a time to increase the popularity of his own political opponent, Kenyatta, just so Mboya would not have any possibility of taking over the government in 1963. In turn, Mboya did all he could to get Odinga ousted as vice president in 1966.

When Mboya was assassinated, radio broadcasts from the Communist countries attempted to blame the Western powers, while Kenya's Vice President Arap Moi put the blame squarely on the Communists.

In less than two weeks after the assassination the Nairobi police charged Nahashon Isaac Njenga Njoroye with the murder of Tom Mboya. By this name it was known immediately that he was a Kikuyu, thus seeming to confirm the Luos' worst thoughts—that there was a political plot to prevent non-Kikuyus from filling important posts in the government.

Njenga was tried, convicted and sentenced to death by hanging. Nevertheless, the trial opened up more questions than it answered. For one thing, despite the fact that the assassination took place within view of a crowded downtown street, not one witness came forward to identify the assassin. Most of the evidence was circumstantial. Both the public and the police seemed not to believe that the assassin had acted alone. There was even doubt whether Njenga was the one that pulled the trigger. Phrases such as "the big man" and "the others" appeared as veiled references in court.

Two theories took shape after the trial and Vice President Arap Moi was busy promoting one of them. According to him foreign interests, perhaps acting through members of the KPU opposition party, were very much involved. Supporters of this viewpoint note that Njenga stated to the police that he had been given the gun by a member of the KPU. They also stress that at one time he went to school in Bulgaria, and it was common knowledge that Mboya was hostile to leftist elements in or out of Africa.

The second theory is based on the supposition that the anti-Mboya people in the ruling KANU ordered the assassination, and to lend support to this, it is noted that Njenga once worked as a bodyguard for a former mayor of Nairobi who was a rival of Mboya's for national leadership. Statements Mboya made to his friends a couple of months before his death made it clear that Mboya felt in danger from enemies within his own party, enemies that he thought were getting "nervous and desperate" as a result of President Kenyatta's plans to hold a general election later in the year. This belief was strengthened by the fact that in December 1967 a bizarre incident took place. The army sentry guard stationed outside Mboya's house suddenly began firing at Mboya. When pressed, the official explanation was that the sentry had lost his reason.

President Kenyatta tried to heal the animosities

that naturally arose after Mboya's death by appointing a Luo friend of Mboya's to succeed him as minister of economic planning and development. However, political analysts have pointed out that besides the loss to the country of his great technical and organizational skills, the Cabinet lost a member who always managed to push through needed but unpopular legislation. The main effect of the assassination was that in removing Tom Mboya from the Kenya political scene, those who engineered his death eliminated the only popular figure whose energy, vision and ability were in any way a mirror of Jomo Kenyatta. In other words, the strictly political question of whether or not Tom Mboya would succeed Kenyatta as president of Kenya was settled by an assassin's bullet—conclusive as far as stopping Mboya, but as to who ordered the assassination, the jury is still out□

Opposite: Senator John F. Kennedy with Kenya's Tom Mboya (R) and Mboya's brother, Alphonse Okuku, at a 1960 press conference in Hyannis Port, Massachusetts

Tom Mboya, 1960

Above: Mboya as a sportsman

Below: Mboya disclosed that he had been taking
instruction in the Roman Catholic faith preparatory
to his January 1962 wedding to Pamela Odede,
daughter of a former Mau Mau detainee, Walter Odede

Wearing a ceremonial Kenyan hat, Jomo Kenyatta,
president of the Kenya African National Union
(KANU) attended the 1962 Constitutional Conference
in London with Tom Mboya (R), general secretary
of the party

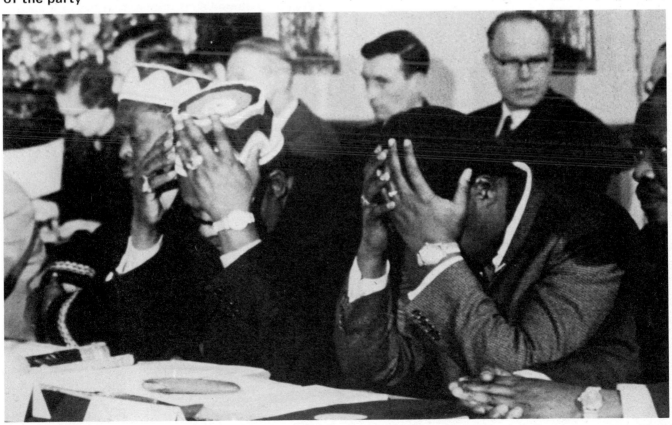

Above: A jubilant Kenyatta (R) and Mboya celebrate after hearing the news that their KANU party claimed victory in the nine-day general elections in 1963. Opposition tribalists and racialists had wanted a regional form of control as opposed to the central government policy of the KANU

Below: After being sworn in as the first prime minister of Kenya, Jomo Kenyatta (2nd R), with some of his newly installed cabinet ministers. (L–R) Tom Mboya, justice and constitutional affairs minister; Oginga Odinga, minister for home affairs; R. Achieng Oneko, minister for information; Kenyatta, and James S. Gichuru, finance minister

Nahashon Isaac Njenga Njoroye, the assassin

After being shot while leaving a Nairobi drugstore, Mboya was rushed to a hospital where he shortly died of a chest wound

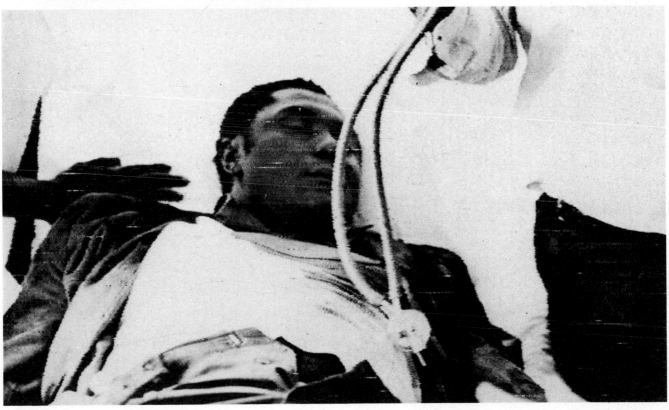

Opposite: Alphonse Mboya, brother of the
slain minister, comforts the widow outside
her Nairobi home

Pamela Mboya weeps over her husband's body

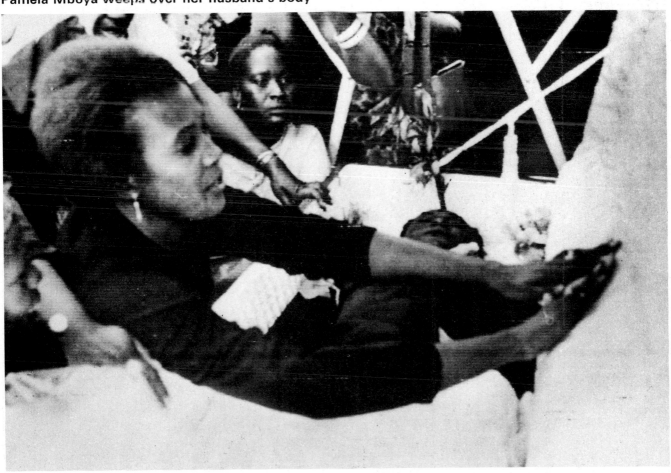

HIS MAJESTY FAISAL BIN ABDULAZIZ

Born 1905 Riyadh, Saudi Arabia
Died March 25, 1975 Ri'Assa Palace, Riyadh, Saudi Arabia

Gained early experience in diplomatic and military affairs; served as Saudi Arabia's foreign minister from the 1930s through to the 1960s when he replaced his brother as Saudi Arabia's king

Assassin:
Prince Faisal Bin Musaed Bin Abdulaziz, 27-year-old nephew of the king

The Saud dynasty dominated the Arabian Peninsula for over 150 years before it was driven out of most of the area by stronger tribes. However, under the leadership of Faisal's father, Abdulaziz, popularly known as Ibn Saud, the Saud reconquest of the region began in 1901. Faisal was trained early and well for his eventual leadership role. At the age of 14 he was selected to go on a diplomatic mission to England. His father then placed him in a combat position where he was able to demonstrate his military prowess. While still a teenager Faisal led 45,000 Bedouin troops against his father's rivals and was so successful that he was put in command of one of Ibn Saud's armies. In the 1920s the Sauds won control of Jidda and the holy cities of Mecca and Medina, in the process driving out Sharif Hussein, the great-grandfather of the present king of Jordan. By 1932 Ibn Saud was able to amalgamate the conquered territories into the kingdom now known as Saudi Arabia.

For most of the 1930s through 1960s Faisal was foreign minister of Saudi Arabia and became well known to the Western world and its leaders. But when his father was near death, it was no surprise that the traditional ways were followed and Faisal's older brother Saud was designated to succeed Ibn Saud. For the next ten years King Saud managed to squander much of the nation's oil royalties on extraordinary luxuries for himself and his one hundred wives and concubines.

Extravagances such as using half the electrical power in Riyadh to air-condition his palaces moved the country close to bankruptcy. Finally the Royal Council decided that the king would have to be replaced and Faisal assumed control. Saud was sent off to a luxurious exile in Greece, and Faisal began to reorganize the government. Royal allowances were cut, royal princes were married off in wholesale lots of four at a time to save on wedding expenses, and the nation was put on a respectable financial basis.

Although well acquainted with Western life-styles, Faisal proceeded slowly to introduce change into the essentially feudal society of his country in order not to offend the religious elders. He himself was deeply religious and lived a relatively ascetic personal life. Such was not always the case with the 3,000 royal princes and 4,000 royal women. This large regal family was subject to much intrigue and plotting, but Faisal, in the tradition of Arab rulers, was the most expert intriguer of them all and managed to successfully play off one against the other in order to maintain his control.

Through most of the 1960s Faisal displayed an openly aggressive attitude toward Egypt in Yemen. When the military overthrew the theocratic government of the Imam, in 1962, a civil war had broken out in which Saudi Arabia supported the anti-republican Imam and Egypt backed the new government. The civil war lasted until after the Six Day War of 1967, when Egypt withdrew its military forces from Yemen and received Saudi Arabian financial aid to make up for its losses. After Nassar's death in 1970 Saudi Arabia moved toward closer relations with Anwar Sadat, and in the last days of the October 1973 war against Israel, Faisal turned almost certain Arab defeat on the battlefield into a geopolitical victory by instituting the Arab oil embargo. Since 1973, oil revenues have been estimated at between $20 and $29 billion a year, and even though he had shown some interest in introducing certain economic and social reforms, Faisal was still debating at the time of his death whether or not to proceed with a proposed $150 billion development program. He was apparently deeply troubled by the thought of hundreds of thousands of Western technicians and workers descending on his backward nation of about five million people.

In foreign policy Faisal followed a conservative pro-Western position that made him extremely unpopular among Arab radicals who considered him a reactionary tyrant. However, as these same Arab leaders came to realize that Faisal was, or could be, the source of enormous subsidies for their various projects, their criticism of him softened. In addition to his vast oil revenues Faisal had two other bases for attracting widespread support. The Moslem holy places were within his territory, thus gaining for his policies the support of conservative religious elements throughout the Arab world; more importantly, Faisal was a rabid anti-Zionist who was determined to liberate Arab Jerusalem. So his immense oil wealth, together with his Holy War attitude toward Israel, combined to make him the foremost leader in the Arab world.

On the morning of the Prophet Mohammed's birthday King Faisal was preparing to meet with a special Kuwaiti delegation in the private reception room of the Ri'Assa Palace. On that particular day he was to conduct a *majlis*, an open court, for sheiks and shepherds alike. As the Kuwaitis made their way past the white-robed palace guard, armed with machine guns and gold swords, a young man stepped out of the crowd to greet the oil minister of Kuwait. The young mustached man, who had his long Western-styled hair hidden by the flowing Arab *kafiyeh*, waited outside the reception room, talking with the oil minister, who was a former classmate of his. When the Kuwaitis were ushered into the presence of the king, the young man followed them in the reception line. As the king lowered his head to accept the customary kiss on the tip of his nose, the assassin reached beneath his cloak, drew a revolver and shot the king twice in the head. He fired a third time but missed and then threw the gun on the floor as he shouted: "Now my brother is avenged!" The King was rushed to a nearby hospital, but he was already dead—one of the bullets had struck him in the brain.

The young assassin was quickly identified as Prince Faisal Bin Musaed Bin Abdulaziz, a 27-year-old nephew of the king, who had spent most of the previous ten years in the United States. In 1966 Prince Faisal had studied English at San Francisco State College and later had studied at the University of Colorado where he was known more for his gambling and drinking than for his scholarship. In 1969 he and his blonde movie actress girl friend had been arrested on charges of selling fifty-two tablets of LSD and fifteen grams of hashish to an undercover agent. Apparently only intercession by the Saudi Embassy resulted in their release after they pleaded no contest to the drug charge. Although barely graduating from college, Prince Faisal was accepted as a graduate student in political science at the University of California at Berkeley in 1973. At Berkeley he wore his hair long, maintained a respectable position in the drug society and associated with militant Arab students. There he often aired his increasingly radical ideas and spoke openly of his embarrassment at being part of the Saudi royal family. In 1974 Prince Faisal returned to Saudi Arabia, becoming an instructor at Riyadh University where he was reportedly regarded as emotionally unstable enough to require psychiatric treatment. One of his more publicized actions was his rejection of the annual stipend of between $12,000 and $15,000 to which he was entitled as one of the 3,000 royal princes.

Immediately after the assassination the Saudi government branded him as "mentally deranged", but within a week there was an official reversal, and he was declared sane and fit to stand trial. Much effort was expended to determine his real motive. Some rumored explanations stressed his interest in radical Arab politics while studying abroad. Authorities were also concerned about a stamp on his passport indicating that at some point Prince Faisal, without his family's knowledge, had visited East Germany. Another rumor had it that the young prince was part of a conspiracy involving anti-Saudi elements in the military. (In 1969 King Faisal had discovered such a plot that had resulted in the arrest of sixty of his own air force officers.) Perhaps the assassin wanted revenge for the fact that the king refused to allow him to travel abroad because of his previous arrest record in the U.S. Still another theory, and the one championed by the radical Arab press in some countries, was that Prince Faisal was a tool of the United States Central Intelligence Agency.

But the Saudi security investigation came up with an explanation that tied into the young man's own words at the moment of his deed. According to this theory the motive was revenge for the death of his brother Prince Khalid, who had been killed nine years earlier by Saudi police while leading an attack of Moslem fundamentalists on a new Riyadh television station. (Religious fundamentalists believe that the Koranic bar on human images should include a ban on television.) At the time, Prince Faisal had pleaded to the king for the execution of the policeman who had fired the shots, but his appeal was to no avail.

Because he was considered mentally competent Prince Faisal received the standard penalty for murder—public beheading. The verdict of guilty was announced to a crowd of thousands immediately before the executioner swung down his gold-hilted sword. The assassin's head was displayed for a time on a wooden stake before being removed by ambulance with the rest of the body for burial.

According to a prearranged plan, the Saud family named Crown Prince Khalid the successor to his assassinated half-brother, King Faisal. King Khalid thereupon selected as his deputy prime minister Prince Fahad, a half-brother and member of the most powerful section of the Saudi family—the Sudeiri Seven (seven sons whose mother, a woman of the Sudeiri family, was the favorite of founding King Ibn Saud's three hundred wives).

Domestically, modernization will probably proceed at a somewhat more rapid pace than before, while Saudi Arabia's foreign policy continues on the course set by the murdered King Faisal—violently anti-Israel and fully committed to the use of her vast oil resources as an instrument of international diplomatic pressure□

Above: King Faisal meeting with U.S. Secretary of State
Henry Kissinger at the Ri'Assa Palace, February 1975

Below: Faisal, trying his hand at
marksmanship

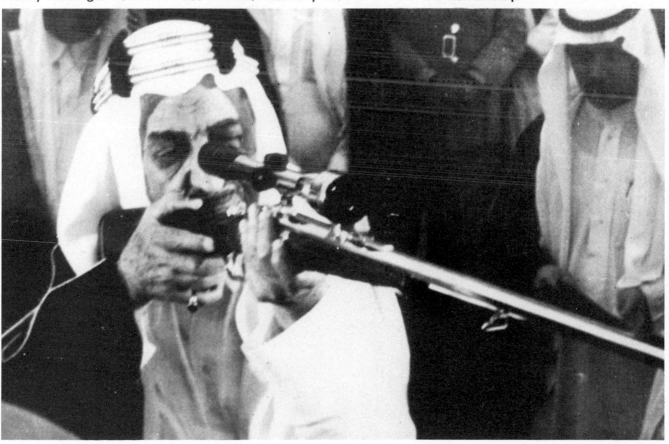

Faisal (L) with his half-brother Crown Prince Khalid

Above: Prince Faisal Bin Musaed Bin Abdulaziz, the nephew and assassin of his uncle, King Faisal

Above right: The assassin as pictured in a University of Colorado 1971 yearbook

Christine Surma, an actress and former fiancée of Prince Faisal, told newsmen that she was shocked by the slaying. She described the Prince as "a genius—a very brilliant man".

Above: The shrouded body of the assassinated king as Arab leaders mourn his death. (R–L) Algerian President Boumedienne, Egyptian President Anwar Sadat, Qatar ruler El Thani and Yasser Arafat of the Palestine Liberation Organization

Below: Surrounded by members of the royal family, the new King Khalid (with hand extended palm downward) weeps over the shrouded body of King Faisal before the March 26 burial at the Royal Cemetery

King Khalid, successor to Faisal

Deputy Prime Minister Fahad, powerful member of the Sudeiri branch of the Saud family

INDEX

Apte, Narayan, 94, 96, 97, 103, 105
Azad, Maulana, 101
Badge, Digambar, 94, 96, 97, 105
Gandhi, Mohandas Karamchand
  (Mahatma), 94, 95, 96, 97, 98, 99, 100,
  101, 102, 103, 104, 105
Gandhi, Mrs. Acq, 101
Gandhi, Sita, 102, 103
Gandhi, Tara, 102, 103

Godse, Gopal, 96, 105
Godse, Nathuram Vinayak, 94, 96, 97, 103,
  105
Karkare, Vishnu, 94, 96, 97, 105
Kistayya, Shankar, 94, 96, 97, 105
Nayar, Dr. Sushila, 101
Nehru, Pandit Jawaharlal, 99, 104, 105
Pahwa, Mandanlal, 94, 96, 97, 105
Savarkar, Vinayak, 94, 97, 105

MAHATMA GANDHI

Dulles, Allen, 110
Eisenhower, President, 110
Gat, Captain, 111
Hammarskjold, Dag, 111
Huyghe, Colonel, 111
Kasavubu, Joseph, 109, 110, 111, 113, 120
Leopold II, 108
Lumumba, Patrice Emery, 106, 107, 108,
  109, 110, 111, 112, 115, 116, 117, 118, 119

Lumumba, Patrice, Jr., 110, 120
Lumumba, Mrs. Pauline, 110, 121
Mobuto, Colonel Joseph, (Sese Seko), 110,
  111, 114, 115, 116, 120
Mpolo, Maurice, 110, 117, 118
Munongo, Godefroid, 110, 111, 114, 118
Nkrumah, Kwame, 109
Okito, Joseph, 110, 117, 118
Stanley, Henry M., 108
Tshombe, Moise, 109, 110, 111, 114

PATRICE LUMUMBA

Balaguer, President, 128
Betancourt, President Romulo, 126
Bissell, Richard, 126
Castro, Fidel, 125
Cedeño, Pedro Livio, 122, 126, 128
Cooley, Representative Harold, 125
Cruz, Captain Zacarias de la, 128, 135
Díaz, Brigadier General Juan Tomas, 122,
  125, 126, 134, 135
Eastland, Senator James, 125
Ellender, Senator Allen, 125
Estrella, Salvador, 122, 126
Fernandez, General Román, 122, 126
Gabor, Zsa Zsa, 125, 131
Galindez, Dr. Jesus de, 125
García, Amado, 127, 128
Guerrero, Lieutenant Amado García, 122,
  126, 134
Hull, Cordell, 132

Imbert, General Antonio, 122, 126, 128
Kennedy, President John F., 126, 127
Molina, Rafael Leonidas Trujillo, see
  Trujillo, Rafael
Novak, Kim, 125, 131
Pastoriza, Roberto, 122, 126
Pimental, Huascar Antonia Tejeda, 122, 126
Roosevelt, Franklin Delano, Jr., 125
Rubirosa, Porfirio, 136
Rusk, Dean, 126
Salazar, Dr., 124
Spellman, Francis Cardinal, 133
Tío, Luis Amiama, 122, 126, 128
Trujillo, Dona Maria Martinez de, 129
Trujillo, Flor de Oro, 136
Trujillo, Hector B., 128, 129
Trujillo, Jose Arismende, 128
Trujillo, Rafael, 122, 123, 124, 125, 126,
  127, 128, 129, 130, 132, 133, 137
Trujillo, Rafael, Jr., 125, 128, 130, 131
Vasquez, Antonia de la Muza, 122, 126, 134

RAFAEL TRUJILLO

Can, Ngo Dinh, 147
De Gaulle, General, 141
Diem, President Ngo Dinh, 138, 139, 140,
  141, 142, 144, 145, 146
Harkins, General Paul, 141
Lalouette, Roger, 141
Le Thuy, Ngo Dinh, 145

Lodge, Henry Cabot, 141, 142
Maneli, Mieczylaw, 141
Nhu, Madame, 140, 141, 142, 145, 146, 147
Nhu, Ngo Dinh, 140, 141, 142, 143, 146,
  147
Radford, Admiral Arthur W., 144
Taylor, General Maxwell, 144
Thuc, Archbishop Ngo Dinh, 140, 141

NGO DINH DIEM